The protection of industrial designs
A practical guide for businessmen and industrialists

THE PROTECTION OF INDUSTRIAL DESIGNS

A practical guide for businessmen and industrialists

G. Myrants, Dip.EE, ARMTC, MSE, Grad.IEAust., FIL

McGRAW-HILL Book Company (UK) Limited

London · New York · St Louis · San Francisco · Auckland · Bogotà
Düsseldorf · Johannesburg · Madrid · Mexico · Montreal
New Delhi · Panama · Paris · São Paulo · Singapore · Sydney
Tokyo · Toronto

Published by

McGraw-Hill Book Company (UK) Limited
Maidenhead · Berkshire · England

British Library Cataloguing in Publication Data

Myrants, G
  The protection of industrial designs.
  1. Design protection—Great Britain
  I. Title
  346'.41'0484   KD1345   77-30040

ISBN 0-07-084495-X

1234 JWA 7987

PRINTED AND BOUND IN GREAT BRITAIN

Contents

1. Introduction to registration system   1
There is an ever increasing demand for good designs
and these can be protected by way of a registration
procedure. A full explanation of the meaning of an
industrial design is followed by a practical comparison of
design registrations with other forms of industrial property protection and guidance as to if and when a design
registration is preferable.

2. Registrability   13
The qualification of a design for protection by the registration procedure is explained systematically with the
aid of numerous practical examples of commonly
encountered products and only sufficient reference to
the legal whys and wherefores to make the discussion
intelligible. In addition to defining the features to be
possessed by registrable designs and articles embodying
those designs, a description is included of exempting
provisions permitting the protection of certain designs
that are otherwise barred from registration. All the
circumstances are covered that should enable a prospective applicant to decide on the feasibility of a design
registration.

outline is given of the principal differences and how to decide where one should file abroad.

This is probably the first thorough study that has ever been published for businessmen on this baffling subject. Copyright protection for industrial designs is explained, compared and evaluated from a commercial point of view, with special emphasis on where there is no overlap with the design law. Valuable advice is included in the form of a checklist for safeguarding copyright. A sample copyright licence is also given.

For the sake of completeness, examples are given of passing-off actions, private protection procedures and secrecy and know-how agreements, with a detailed set of heads of agreement for a know-how licence.

The author has gazed into a crystal ball and indicated where changes might one day be made.

Illustrations

List of items of manufacture referred to in the text

Preface

Designs, in the sense of eye-appealing industrial creations as opposed to mechanical contrivances, are capable of protection in the UK by a registration procedure, which has been in existence for almost one and a half centuries. For a like period, registered designs have been the subject of discussions and disputes in and out of court. Yet, to this day, designs are the least well understood of the possessions collectively known as industrial property rights. Patents, registered trade marks and copyright are rights with the meaning and advantages of which many people are at least vaguely familiar but the availability of design protection often comes as a complete surprise to manufacturers and importers, distributors and retailers—the very people who would benefit by being able to suppress unfair competition or who, in the knowledge of someone else's design rights, could take steps to avoid infringement. This lack of understanding is particularly unfortunate in the case of a business founded on the basis of a new or improved product as its only real asset.

Considerable confusion on this subject sometimes also exists in the legal profession, particularly when it comes to the practical aspects of obtaining design protection and advising on the desirability of acquiring a design registration in preference to relying on the law of artistic copyright. Commentaries published on the subject throughout the years have been few and far between, especially those which do not tend to be too complicated for the layman. Experience shows time and again that businessmen and product managers want something other than legally-worded explanations which are carefully supported by quotations from reported judgments; they are more interested in practical information presented to them in plain terms in relation to the problems which they encounter in their everyday work.

My book was inspired by a request for a collection of the advice that I have given to clients and overseas associates on design and allied matters in my many years of practice. It seemed that there was a scarcity of reading matter on this topic, so I began not only to summarize the theory, but also to consider and record the subject from a commercial point of view to bridge the gap that undoubtedly exists between design law and the practical issues. While I was tempted to devote much more space than I have done to theoretical questions and quotations from judgments, with a table of cases as is usual in law books so that the work might serve as a comprehensive commentary or textbook, I have decided in favour of preserving the simplicity of the book. For the same reason, I have not traced the history of design protection; I have not gone to great lengths in construing the statutes and analysing their defects; nor have I attempted to explain the intentions of the legislators and make exhaustive suggestions for improving the law. Instead, I have concentrated on the original intention of correlating available practical information and experience in the form of a reference manual that is addressed to the layman—the man in industry or commerce who wishes to know what protection is presently available and how he should go about acquiring it—with just enough excerpts from the law and examples from decided cases to enable a better practical understanding of the various aspects to be obtained. Particular attention has been paid to artistic copyright in so far as it affects industrial designs.

This work should also be of interest to the many foreign patent attorneys needing a simplified explanation of British design law and practice for the benefit of any of their clients desiring protection in the UK, to solicitors who conduct a general practice and to law students who require a general, though by no means superficial, review of the subject, it being understood that they must not hang on my every word. Academic and procedural questions of little or no interest to manufacturers, merchants or industrial information officers have been omitted. There are also no footnotes listing decided cases, it being deemed sufficient to mention elucidating judgments in the main text without specific identification. Particular care has been given to compiling a comprehensive index so as to avoid excessive use of cross-references within related sections of the book.

If I have succeeded in presenting a readable general survey and guide on matters affecting the protection of industrial designs, the reader will realize the advisability of continuing to seek first-hand professional advice in specific cases of difficulty or in disputes. A book can never be an adequate substitute for first hand guidance from a specialist; but it is hoped that I have managed to provide an insight into the considerations that may have perplexed manufacturers in the past, so that they will now be better equipped to compete with the continued flood of imported products and to take precautions against infringing foreign design registrations with their exported products.

Acknowledgements

Figure 5.1 is reproduced from the *Report of the Departmental Committee on Industrial Designs*, cmnd 1808, HMSO, 1962.

Figures 3.3, 3.4, 3.6, 3.7 are reproductions of official forms published by HMSO, issued by the Designs Registry and filled in with information furnished by the author.

Figures 2.1, 3.11, 3.12, 5.2, 5.4, 5.7, 5.8, 5.9, 5.10, 5.11, 7.1, 7.2, and 7.3 are illustrations reproduced from *Reports of Patent, Trade Mark and other Cases* published periodically by the Patent Office.

Figure 3.2 was prepared for the author by Algar, Gibson & Rose, London, a firm of specialist draughtsmen who also assisted in redrawing some of the previously mentioned reproductions.

The other figures and all the tables are from originals prepared by the author.

In the text, quotations of judges' comments are all taken from either *Reports of Patent, Trade Mark and other Cases*, or from unreported judgments as laid open to public inspection at the National Reference Library of Science and Invention, Holborn Division.

The extracts and illustrations from official documents are the subject of Crown Copyright and are used with the permission of the Controller of Her Majesty's Stationery Office.

1. *Introduction to registration system*

1.1 Industrial designing

The execution of designs is an art that has been practised for thousands of years, although in the distant past the artists responsible for the works which we now choose to refer to as 'industrial designs' were not concerned with the definition of this term, and least of all with the problem of how to protect their works against copying. Originally, industrial designs were conceived while forming and embellishing everyday articles of use; these were practically the only goods made industrially at that time, that is to say, made by some mechanized process of multiplication as distinct from being fashioned by hand. But even with the advent of mechanization, it is doubtful that the authors of designs were troubled by thoughts of preventing unfair competition by trade rivals. Attractive designs were conceived as a matter of pride in one's work and for the pleasure they would eventually give to the purchaser. Utility was, and is to this day, more important than are aesthetic considerations. Essentially, a product must fulfil its required purpose; a pleasing appearance is of secondary but by no means insignificant importance.

For centuries industrial designs have also been executed by manufacturers who consciously seek to enhance the sales appeal of their products by way of ornamentation so as to gain an advantage over their competitors. Nevertheless, functional considerations have tended to predominate in most cases. Very few people would, for example, today choose a motor car solely for its shape; its appearance is not considered in preference to its performance. Similarly, a shirt is not selected because it looks attractive if it does

1

not also fit properly, nor a shovel for its pleasing shape rather than its size. There are, of course, several exceptions. The attractiveness of the pattern on wallpaper or a dining room carpet is usually decisive when making a choice, no matter how practical the quality of the material might be.

However, only in comparatively recent times has industrial designing been really intensified, encouraged by a variety of factors including the desirability of exploiting wider markets, the existence of fiercer competition at home and abroad, the availability of more media for advertising and display, the discovery of very many new processes and materials lending themselves to intricate but inexpensive shaping and ornamentation and, not least, a higher level of education. It is probable that a more widespread appreciation of the arts resulting from general education has been chiefly responsible for a greater demand by consumers for something better than mere utilitarian goods. This, in turn, has led to the establishment of more design faculties at colleges; also to the creation of organizations such as the Design Council and bodies that recommend meritorious designs by granting awards and seals of approval.

1.2   Legislation

Legislators in this country and abroad have not been slow in affording protection to the authors of new industrial designs as a reward for their labours. The current law governing registered designs is the Registered Designs Act 1949. Unfortunately, although a system of registration has been in existence in the UK since 1839, British manufacturers have for some reason been comparatively reluctant to avail themselves of the benefits of design registrations. This is surprising in a nation that is highly developed industrially and prides itself on possessing resourceful inventors and innovators. In order to preserve their position and at the same time help solve the country's recurrent balance-of-payments problem, British industries would have been expected to rely on all the protection they can possibly obtain from the law to monopolize the market for locally designed and locally made consumer goods and luxury articles against the ever increasing competition presented by imported copies. Instead, British manufacturers have tended to give an almost clear run to foreign products. Judging from officially published figures, we are gradually approaching the time when the British will be outnumbered by foreigners in applying for design registrations in the UK. In 1960, there were 24 foreign to every 100 British applicants. Only 10 years later, the proportion had climbed to 65 foreign applicants for every 100 British applicants. Consequently, manufacturers in this country are finding not only that their production programmes are becoming increasingly restricted by having to avoid infringement of the designs registered by foreign competitors both here and abroad but also that their own new products can be too readily copied.

1.3 The registration system

Designs are a form of industrial property that can be protected by a registration procedure, exploited to the advantage of the registered proprietor and his licensees, or abused by competitors—all in much the same way as inventions and trade marks can be. A general comparison between designs and other forms of protection appears later in this chapter. In the UK, with which this book is primarily concerned, the right given by a design registration is a monopoly and can be infringed without copying having taken place. The position differs in some other countries (for example, in Germany, where a design registration is infringed only if there has been copying), and it is as well to remember this. There are laws, rules and official practices governing very many aspects of industrial design registrations, and where there are laws there are interpretations rendered by court decisions, followed by amending laws and still further decisions with consequential changes in official practice. All these are of the greatest interest to practitioners because the law and procedure obviously influence the advice given by design registration agents to their clients.

1.4 Case law and bibliography

Since the present book is not intended to be a learned exposition for use as a legal textbook, decided cases have for the most part not been identified and analysed. It is unfortunate that many interesting and elucidating decisions and rulings, especially by the Registrar of Designs and his examiners, cannot be adequately reported to the public because particulars of refused applications for design registrations must remain secret. The judgments in leading known cases can be found in *Reports of Patent, Design, Trade Mark and other Cases*, published periodically by the Patent Office, and in *Fleet Street*

Patent Law Reports, published periodically by Fleet Street Patent Law Reports Limited, London. One or two excellent legal commentaries have also been written, the best-known being by Michael Fysh and entitled *Russell-Clarke on Copyright in Industrial Designs* (fifth edn, Sweet and Maxwell, London, 1974). It is the bible of professional advisers on the subject and anyone who wishes to study design law more deeply can do no better than read it. Another good textbook is *Patents for Inventions and the Protection of Industrial Designs* by T. A. Blanco White (fourth edn, Stevens and Sons, London, 1974). Attention is also directed to the valuable investigations, analyses, and criticisms of the industrial design law contained in the *Report of the Departmental Committee on Industrial Designs* presented to Parliament in August 1962 and published by HMSO. Finally, it should be mentioned that designs and their relationship to artistic copyright are discussed in *Copinger and Skone James on Copyright* (eleventh edn, by E. P. Skone James, MA, Sweet and Maxwell, London, 1971).

1.5   Good designs

A good design is many things, but two qualities are essential: a well-designed article should be pleasing in appearance and it should fulfil its intended purpose properly. The design may or may not be a form of artistic expression; this becomes of interest in a later chapter of this book dealing with copyright. We are here concerned with articles which, as distinct from works of art, serve an important function in addition to that of being displayed for the appraisal of art lovers. An industrial design is intended to improve the visual qualities of useful articles for the benefit of consumers, without sacrificing utility, safety and economy in production—a so-called marriage between artistic and functional considerations.

In the UK there is an officially sponsored organization to advise on good designs, namely the Design Council which has offices in London and Glasgow. The Council can be of tremendous help to manufacturers who wish to improve their products for the home or export market by putting them in touch with the most suitable designers for employment on a permanent, freelance or consultancy basis. The Council also promotes good designs by displaying them at the Design Centre and including them in *Design Index*, which is an illustrated record of contemporary products provided for inspection by visitors. Foreign purchasers and agents and British trade representatives abroad are kept advised of new articles included in *Design Index*, which is also used for selecting products for overseas exhibitions. A periodical publication, *Design*, is published by the Design Council to inform British and overseas readers about noteworthy British products and the many aspects of industrial designing.

1.6 Functional attributes disregarded

It has been stated in the preceding section that a well designed article must do its job well. In everyday language, we use the noun 'design' to denote any idea that is to be executed in any manner. It is important, however, to understand that the term 'industrial design' with which the Registered Designs Act is concerned has nothing to do with that which is achieved by the act of contriving or devising in the sense of planning a mechanical construction for an article so that it will operate properly or fulfil an intended functional purpose. Such a mechanical construction or contrivance or device is in the domain of patent protection if inventive ingenuity had to be exercised to bring it about. Instead, the industrial design to which the Designs Act is applicable, and in fact confined, is a plan, scheme or idea for decorative work to be carried into effect by industrial resources or expedients. The creation must possess features that can be perceived by the eye and are judged and appreciated by the eye. It is only these visual aspects for which design registrations cater. Function must be left out of consideration. What is more, it will be explained later that registrable designs are those which are applied or given to articles, hopefully with a view to influencing the choice of customers. If there is no article, the design is not registrable.

Assuming that a prospective purchaser has decided on the precise function that he wishes the product to perform and he has narrowed down his choice to a few such products which, so he believes, will carry out the function satisfactorily, his final selection will invariably be influenced not only by price but also by the appearance of the articles—by the eye-catching features, such as shape, colour, pattern and ornamentation. He may be attracted to an article having a clean geometrical or streamlined outline, or an artistically executed or neat appearance, or because it is grotesque, or simply because it looks different from the article that he and his friends have owned previously. The statute governing the protection of industrial designs by a registration procedure is intended to deal with all these eye-appealing features (not efficiency in operation or use, certainly not features that cannot be seen and assessed by the eye), features of appearance provided additional to the basic functional requirements to be fulfilled by the article.

1.7   Designs in relation to patentable inventions

By reason of ignorance on the subject, registered designs have, at best, been wrongly regarded as the poor relation of patents. Indeed, manufacturers and importers who may have heard about patents are invariably unaware of the availability of design protection or the risks that they run by copying a competitor's article which might not be patented but is protected by a design registration. Even professional advisers who are preoccupied with patent considerations have been known to overlook the possible existence of design registrations or the advisability of obtaining design protection for their clients. This is not surprising if one bears in mind that some books on the protection of industrial property dismiss designs in a single paragraph. If industry could be better informed about the practical issues, it would soon realize that a design registration is vitally important as a useful adjunct to patent protection or as a substitute in cases where patent protection is not obtainable for one reason or another; the opportunity of securing valuable monopolies would not be lost and fewer manufacturers would find themselves in the alarming situation of inadvertently infringing a competitor's rights.

To explain the difference between a patent for an invention and a registration for a design, it is convenient to regard a patent as being granted for some novel and inventive functional aspect which can usually be concisely defined in words, possibly by referring to the mechanical characteristics of an article or its function or the result that is to be achieved—for example, an electric circuit, an engine or mechanism, a particular composition for a chemical preparation, a new step in a manufacturing process, a novel machine or instrument, or an improved method of testing materials. A registrable design, as has been stated, is not concerned with function at all, only with the appearance of an article as brought about by features of shape and/or decoration—this being by far more difficult to define even with the help of pictorial representations. Patents are rarely granted validly for particular shapes or decorations unless some new principle of construction is also involved or a novel shape is developed for a product for unobvious functional reasons. Design registrations are certainly not valid if the designs consist only of features of shape dictated by functional considerations.

1.8 Design registration or patent?

It should therefore be rare for a manufacturer or his adviser to be in any doubt in choosing between a design registration or a patent. More often than not, a choice is not open to him. The nature of the new article of manufacture or the nature of the innovation in respect of an old article should decide the question for him. If the article is such that it can be made in various forms or with different decorative effects without departing from some underlying novel concept that has been developed, a patent application is clearly advisable, although a design application should preferably also be filed for the preferred form and decoration of the article. Take, for example, a tea trolley which, for the first time ever, has been constructed so that it can be readily converted into a coffee table. The inventor will obviously wish to protect the new principle of construction, say a hinged flap and foldable supporting struts in combination with the trolley top. A registered design would protect only the particular shape of the tea trolley and/or its shape after conversion to a coffee table, but this is not enough. In order that competitors can ultimately be prevented from making or marketing convertible tea trolleys as such, no matter what their appearance might be, a patent application will be essential.

If an article possesses no underlying novel inventive concept, only a design application will be feasible. Examples of this are conventional wallpaper or carpeting bearing an original pattern, an armchair with a newly shaped backrest and an ornamental candlestick. Less frequently, one also encounters articles which cannot possibly have more than one basic shape in order to function properly, say the interfitting components of a constructional toy. For these, a patent can be considered but a design registration will not afford valid protection. Again, if the novelty resides in a method of manufacture or in a composition where the form of the product is immaterial, a design registration will be out of the question.

1.9 A patent is not stronger

Statistics are sometimes misused to show that, because design registrations are not as common as patents, a design registration is less useful. It is true that markedly fewer designs are granted annually than are patents. This finds an explanation in three main factors. First, only a small number of people in this country know the availability of design protection, whereas more are aware of patents. Second, patents are unrealistically easy to obtain in the UK by reason of statutory limitations to the official examining procedure. It is laid down that a Patent Office examiner can appraise the novelty but not the inventive merit or obviousness of an invention. Questions of inventive ingenuity are considered only later—if and when the grant of a patent is opposed, or the validity of a granted patent is attacked, by a third party. Also, the examiner's novelty search is mostly confined to prior British patent specifications. Foreign specifications and other publications which are readily available in the UK are not covered; nor does the examiner consider instances of prior use. It is not generally realized, therefore, that many patents are invalid and hence unenforcible; they are not worth the paper on which they are printed, except perhaps for their scare value among the uninformed. In contrast, it is believed that nowadays the majority of registered designs is valid. If, as has been proposed, the patent examining procedure in the UK should be made more thorough to embrace questions of obviousness and prior use and to take all locally available printed publications into account, there would not be such a disparity between the numbers of granted patents and design registrations each year, because more patent applications would be refused and abandoned. Manufacturers would then also be encouraged to rely more heavily on useful design protection (rather than spend time and money on a patent application that is destined to fail), with a consequent further increase in the proportion of design registrations to patents. Finally, for a fair comparison of numbers (which has so far never been attempted), it is necessary to disregard the very many patents granted for subjects such as processes, compositions, electric circuits and immovable structures, which are not eligible for protection by the design registration procedure.

One should, therefore, not be misled by numbers; they are not a true basis for comparison. Even if they were, they would not be a guide to comparative strengths of patents and design registrations. Strength has to be judged by the ease with which the patent or design is enforced against offending competitors. In the author's experience with both these forms of industrial property protection, there is a marked tendency towards more respect for design registrations by persons who are familiar with them.

1.10 Design registration and patent?

Whether or not to incur the cost (low though it might be despite heavy increases in government fees throughout the years) of applying for design protection in addition to a patent application is a practical problem which arises quite often. There are occasions when a patent and a registered design can exist side-by-side for one and the same article, but the scope of protection afforded by each is not the same. It is commonly believed that a patent affords broader (as distinct from stronger) protection, although this is by no means always so. For example, any patent that might nowadays be granted for a non-mechanical ashtray is likely to be of such narrow scope that rival manufacturers will find it an easy matter to alter the construction with a view to avoiding patent infringement and yet achieve the same practical effect. However, it is not difficult to see that an ashtray made in some original shape or bearing a new pattern might have a striking novelty that has sales appeal and that will be difficult for a rival manufacturer to copy without infringing a design registration in respect of the ashtray.

One of the disadvantages of the patent system is that Letters Patent take a considerable time to obtain. It is not uncommon to encounter delays of three years from the filing date in the UK, and much longer in many other countries. In the meantime, no patent rights are enforcible against infringers; in fact, no damages are payable at all for infringement that has taken place before official acceptance and publication of the patent application. However, design registrations can be granted in a matter of weeks or months and are therefore enforcible much sooner. This is a forceful argument in favour of supporting a patent application with a design application or perhaps even several design applications.

Going one step further, a patentable invention may concern a comparatively cheaply made article—for example, a toy—for which the tooling costs are not high and for which there may be a demand for only a limited period anyway. An unscrupulous competitor is likely to say to himself: 'Here is a good opportunity for making a quick profit at the inventor's expense; I can legitimately flood the market with my copies and by the time a patent has been granted I shall not mind withdrawing gracefully.' In such a situation, a design registration can prove invaluable because, if the existence of the registration does not in itself discourage the competitor from making and selling his copies at the outset, the registration can be quickly enforced before irreparable harm has been done.

Further, there is the situation where a valid design registration saves the day because a patent for the product is eventually refused or found to be invalid. If someone has developed the proverbial can-opener that is constructed as never before, he can apply for Letters Patent. However, since can-openers belong to what is known as a crowded art where it is difficult (although not impossible) to find something to invent, a can-opener manufacturer who desires to bring out something new to gain an advantage over his competitors will probably have to be content with novel design features as distinct from patentable features. He may have employed a designer to modify his existing product and the designer might have come up with the seemingly patentable idea of combining the can-opener with a bottle-opener and a corkscrew. Let us say that this is new and appeals to the manufacturer who, realizing the commercial potential of such a three-in-one gadget, seeks patent protection. As likely as not, he finds that any patent granted to him for the new product is invalid because the three component parts are old by themselves and their function when aggregated is the same as if the parts had been made and used separately. If the manufacturer was well informed or advised, he would also have applied for a design registration to protect the shape of the gadget. His designer probably incurred considerable time, thought and skill in developing a shape calculated to please the eye—and here the chances are that his design registration will be valid and enforcible.

A typical example of a case tried in the courts was a design registered in respect of an oil filler for motor car engines. A patent that had also been obtained for the filler was declared invalid for want of 'novelty' in the sense in which this term is construed under the Patents Act. The defendants' filler had six sides instead of the four in the registered design, a hinged lid instead of a sliding lid, and holes in the lid that did not appear in the registered design. Nevertheless, the design registration was held to be infringed.

Finally, it is worth mentioning the case of a product that might be validly patented in the UK but its patent cannot be enforced against, say, a competing British mould maker who sells moulding tools to overseas customers, so that the product patented in the UK can be freely made and sold abroad. If there is also a design registration, it can be effectively held against the British mould maker because one of the prohibitions under the Registered Designs Act is the unauthorized production of anything that enables articles bearing the registered design to be made, whether in the UK or elsewhere.

1.11 Designs in relation to trade marks

The difference between an industrial design and a trade mark is far more obvious to the uninitiated and it should not be necessary to go into this aspect in great detail. It suffices to say that a trade mark is a non-descriptive word and/or device that, when applied to articles (either directly or to their packagings), serves to distinguish one manufacturer's or trader's goods from those of another and that can be protected by a registration procedure if certain conditions are fulfilled, whereas a design is concerned with the outward form or appearance of the articles themselves. The choice between a trade mark registration or a design registration does not arise, because their functions are different. There is at least one circumstance, however, in which the practical effects of the protection of designs and trade marks become confusingly similar. This is the case where an original design is devised for a container for some commodity—for example, a bottle for whisky or a squeeze bottle for detergent—and the container design acquires such distinctiveness as a result of extensive and prolonged use that it comes to characterize the quality or property of the commodity within the container in so far as people seeing a container of the design in question will associate its contents with one particular trader or manufacturer. In that event, the design might, long after any registration for it has expired, still be the exclusive property of that trader. The container will be part of the distinctive get-up of the commodity inside it and this get-up, just like an unregistered trade mark, can be the subject of litigation under the law of passing-off. This will be referred to again briefly towards the end of the book (see pp. 193–195).

It is also worth mentioning at this stage that a trade mark, when applied to a particular article, may in some cases qualify for registration as a design. This will really depend on the nature of the trade mark and the nature of the article. The article must be one that serves a principal purpose other than that of just bearing the trade mark, and the trade mark must be one that is decorative and is not excluded from design registration by reason of consisting of words, letters and numerals. Thus, a trade mark of the kind in question will be what is commonly referred to as a device mark or motif—a picture or symbol as distinct from a name or monogram. The article in question can be one of many; more commonly encountered examples that come to mind are coasters, books of matches, ashtrays and carrier bags. These are often given away for advertising purposes, the advertisement consisting principally of the advertiser's picture mark of, say, a spade (used by a well known

Munich brewer) or coloured diagonal stripes (used by the British Airport Authority and its chain of airport shops) or a schooner (used by an international manufacturer of men's toiletries). In all these cases, the picture trade marks are registrable as designs when serving as decorations on useful articles, the fact that they are also protectable as trade marks *per se* being immaterial. However, if the marks are applied to articles such as calendars, leaflets and labels, they are not regarded as registrable designs. A more complete list of excluded articles appears in section 2.6.

1.12 Designs in relation to artistic copyright

The law of industrial designs is regarded as forming part of the law of copyright. The term copyright is also used in the Registered Designs Act 1949, which states that a design registration gives the proprietor the copyright in the design, or, in other words, that copyright subsists in the registered design. However, it is established that a design registration gives an exclusive right—a monopoly—which is infringed irrespective of whether copying has taken place. The word copyright therefore has a peculiar meaning in design law; in any case, it has different connotations for a layman who rather tends to associate the term with original works of art, literature and music. In order that the reader will not be confused, the term copyright has been avoided in this book, except when referring to artistic copyright, which is governed by the Copyright Act 1956 (as amended in 1968). For works created earlier than 1 June 1957, the Copyright Act 1911 still applies.

There is, in fact, considerable overlap between the laws affecting registrable industrial designs and artistic copyright. The relationship between the two laws is of great practical importance, which can be properly appreciated only after registrable industrial designs have been fully explained, so a comparison has been reserved for chapter 7 of this book.

2. *Registrability*

2.1 Definition of a registrable design

The expression 'industrial design' has already been discussed in general terms. To be eligible for registration, a design must possess features of shape, configuration, pattern, or ornament, applied to an article by any industrial process or means—being features that, in the finished article, appeal to and are judged solely by the eye. Many of the words used in this positive definition of a design (there are also negative provisions, discussed later, that have the effect of excluding certain designs and articles from registration) have featured in litigation and we can benefit from studying the meanings of these words because they are important to an applicant in determining whether or not a design is registrable and important to a competitor in deciding whether or not a design was validly registered and is in danger of being infringed by him.

2.2 Design is an idea

By reason of the foregoing definition, a registrable design means one of four, and only four, visible features applied to an article. The design is not the article itself but a feature—an idea or characteristic to be applied or given to an article. However, the design is registrable only when it has been applied or given to the article. If an author has conceived, say, the novel shape of a star, this shape as such cannot be protected by a design registration until it has been transferred from his mind's eye to some article (other than one of the excluded articles referred to later). This is not to say that a design can never be registered before a prototype has been made. On the contrary, the author may mentally embody his idea of a star shape in an article, for example a brooch, prepare complete drawings of the brooch to illustrate all its features of shape and ornament, and then use the drawings as a basis for seeking registration. A registration will be granted provided that the design is to be applied to the brooch by industrial means.

It should be observed that a registrable design has to be applied to 'an' article. Consequently, a decoration to be applied to several articles, for example a floral pattern intended for wallpaper, table linen, carpets, crockery and upholstery material, is protectable only by way of a separate registration for the design when applied to each of these articles.

2.3   Shape, configuration, pattern and ornament

Many knowledgeable minds have been applied unsuccessfully in an attempt to determine the difference between shape and configuration on the one hand, and pattern and ornament on the other hand. In practice, this exercise is not worth the bother. To all intents and purposes, the terms shape and configuration can be paraphrased as the form that an article is to take, for example the three-dimensional shape of a doll, cocktail cabinet, steering wheel, saucepan or yacht, and even the two-dimensional outline of a carton blank before it has been folded and glued to form, say, an Easter-egg box. Pattern and ornament both refer to a decorative effect to be possessed by an article, examples being the two-dimensional pattern on wallpaper, towelling or carpeting, the ornament of lace-work, the pictures applied to a tea-service or a packaging container like a chocolate box, and the three-dimensional ornament of an eternity ring or that of a radiator grill for an automobile. Clearly, some articles possess only novel form (e.g., an ironing board) or only novel decoration (a carpet of known shape but bearing a new floral pattern) and others possess both (a vase of new shape and carrying a new ornamental illustration on its side).

One or more of the four features (but not paraphrased as form and decoration as has been done here for explanatory purposes) must be mentioned in the statement of novelty whenever such a statement is required for a design application. Sometimes a distinction between shape and configuration is all-important. In an infringement action concerning the design of a hot-water bottle having diagonal ribbing over the whole front and back, the defendants pleaded that, since the statement of novelty claimed the feature of shape and configuration, the surface decoration of ribbing should be left out of consideration. The trial judge held that the ribbing was embraced by the term configuration, which is not restricted to outline shape.

In an old case heard in 1894, the defendants were held to infringe a design for a coffin handle plate notwithstanding that the plaintiffs had admitted that the ornament was old. For some unknown reason it was not pleaded that, since the statement of novelty claimed protection only for the now admittedly old ornamental design, as distinct from shape in combination with ornament, the registration should be declared invalid. At that time infringement cases were still heard before a judge and jury. The judge, in his summing up, referred the jury only to the question of infringement. The validity had not come into dispute. It is probable that, unlike the term configuration, 'ornament' does not embrace outline shape; the term 'pattern' certainly does not (see section 3.20).

2.4 Applied industrially

Another requirement in the definition of a registrable design is that it must be applied to an article by any industrial process or means. 'Applied' is a rather inapt description where features of shape are concerned; an article is made in a particular shape or has a shape given to it, but not applied to it. Be that as it may, it is difficult to see that the stipulation of industrial application can exclude anything but unassisted hand application which, in any case, is unlikely to be employed on a commercial scale because of its crude results and because one can never be sure that the same design will be reproduced on each article. Application by a mass-production technique certainly qualifies as 'industrial' every time. By way of interest, it may be mentioned that the Copyright (Industrial Designs) Rules 1957 define, for the purposes of the Copyright Act, the words 'applied industrially' as application to (a) more than fifty articles, all of which do not together constitute a single set, or (b) goods made in lengths or pieces, other than hand-made goods.

Let us consider the case of manually applying a pattern to a piece of pottery or to a fabric. If the workman paints each article in turn, working only from his memory of the original design or from a drawing, obviously nothing that might be called an industrial process is involved; but, if he uses a template to ensure that the hand-painted patterns shall be virtually identical, at least industrial means, if not also an industrial process, will have been employed and the design is registrable.

An interesting decision in a case where the industrial application requirement came into question concerned the design of a petrol filling station; here, the series of operations necessary to the building *in situ* were said to be analogous to those involved in ordinary building and therefore did not constitute the application of a design to an article by an industrial process. A similar decision was handed down in the design of an air-raid shelter to be cast *in situ* from concrete.

2.5 Article

It has already been mentioned that a registrable design is applied or given to an article. 'Design' is not an article but the idea applied to the article or, if you like, the form (shape and configuration) or decoration (pattern and ornament) of the article. The Registered Designs Act also lays down that a design can only be registered in respect of an article or set of articles which must be specified in the application form (for a set of articles see later, but all remarks affecting 'an article' apply equally to each article of a set). It will now be considered exactly what is meant by 'an article'.

The Act actually contains a definition, namely 'An article of manufacture, including any part of an article if that part is made and sold separately'. Leaving parts of articles aside for the moment, the alleged definition of article therefore excludes only objects that are not manufactured—those occurring in nature—but, as soon as a design has been applied industrially even to a naturally occurring object, the resulting product is clearly a manufactured article because the very act of industrially applying a design constitutes a manufacturing step. Consequently, the word 'article', if one were to go strictly by the above quoted definition, would include everything except naturally occurring objects that already have a design by nature.

It will, however, be noted that the so-called definition of 'article' is not particularly helpful because it repeats the word article in what purports to be the definition. It is therefore appropriate to consider whether this word has a more restricted meaning than in normal use. The courts seem to think that it has, namely that it must be something that is preformed, portable, and supplied to the buyer as a finished product. Buildings, including structures such as bridges and railway tunnels, constructed *in situ*, are therefore not 'articles' in respect of which a design can be registered, even if the design were to be applied by a true industrial process (see the end of the preceding section). Prefabricated portable structures (garages, sheds) are not excluded.

2.6 Excluded articles

Apart from permanent buildings and naturally occurring objects that remain unprocessed, it is laid down that designs for specified articles of a mainly literary or artistic character shall not be registered, namely sculptured works, wall plaques, medals, and printed matter. Under this last mentioned heading there appear several examples: book jackets, calendars, certificates, coupons, dressmaking patterns, greeting cards, leaflets, maps, plans, postcards, stamps, trade advertisements, trade forms, cards, and transfers. All these articles are excluded from registration but they are not free to be copied because they are protected by artistic copyright.

It should be noted that not all sculptures are excluded articles. If a sculpture serves, or is even only intended to serve, as a model or pattern to be multiplied by any industrial process (and is so designated in the application form), its design is registrable.

The provisions for excluding the designs of certain articles from registration are applied unduly strictly in some respects. In one unreported case (unreported, because refused applications mostly remain secret), an application for a distinctive fish design to be applied to a wall decoration in the form of a three-dimensional thin hollow plastics moulding having an open back and not unlike a face mask was refused registration on the ground that the design was to be applied to a wall plaque. It is believed that this was wrongly decided by the Registrar because most reputable dictionaries define a 'plaque' as an ornamental plate or tablet, and 'tablet' as a small slab or flat piece of material, these descriptions falling well short of the article that was in question. The case did not go to appeal because the applicant decided to rely on his artistic copyright instead. Had the applicant avoided all reference to 'wall decoration' when first specifying the article in his application form, for example by calling it a 'decorative pattern, primarily for use as a beach toy or jelly mould', it is likely that no official objection would have been raised and that the resultant registration would still have protected the same article when used as a wall decoration. It would also have been possible to obtain a registration in respect of the mould for making the wall decoration.

As an example of where the provisions are interpreted surprisingly generously, one may quote the case of conventionally shaped cartons, such as a chocolate box, in which the novelty resides solely in graphic or photographic illustrations that are printed on the faces of the box. Such designs are officially accepted for registration, despite the prescribed exclusion of printed matter primarily of a literary or artistic character. This attitude is adopted because the box serves a major purpose (namely, to contain chocolates) in addition to that of carrying the printed matter and therefore is not primarily of an artistic character. Wallpaper and playing cards also escape the excluding provisions for this reason. It is even more astounding that wrapping paper is regarded as an acceptable article, the printed matter on it being officially considered as subsidiary to the primary packaging function. One therefore has the extraordinary situation where a designer of a book jacket or trade advertisement is barred from obtaining a design registration but exactly the same design is registrable if the article to which it is applied is referred to as wrapping paper.

The case of trade marks printed on useful articles and regarded as decorations has already been referred to in section 1.11; they fall into the same category as pictures on chocolate boxes.

2.7 Part of an article

Any part of an article that is made and sold separately is included within the statutory definition of an article. The stipulation that it be made separately is really redundant because something that is sold separately has obviously also been separately manufactured, even if it is the retailer who performs the last manufacturing step by, say, severing the article from a string of such articles interconnected by a moulding stem.

Many objects are made in separate parts but in comparatively few cases can the parts be purchased separately. Of course, some manufacturers deliberately offer spare parts for sale but usually such spare parts are also articles in their own right and no questions are asked. In fact, the Designs Registry is generous in interpreting 'part of an article', no doubt realizing that very often a manufacturer is prepared to sell a part by itself to replace a faulty, worn or broken component.

If a manufacturer designs furniture consisting of assembled components, for example a table, and the novelty of the table design resides only in the shape of the legs, then the 'article' to which the design is applied must be regarded as the whole table, even though the legs are made separately, unless he also intends to sell the legs separately. A design registration in respect of a table leg alone obviously affords wider protection than one for the whole table because competitors would be prevented from copying the legs no matter how much they depart from the appearance of the other components of the manufacturer's table. However, the fact remains that a table leg as such can form the subject of a registration only if it is likely to be sold by itself. Here, therefore, we have an example of how the manner of eventual commercial exploitation is a determining factor in deciding the registrability of a design.

2.8 Part of the shape of an article

Although an applicant is compelled to name in his application the entire article in only a portion of which the novel design may actually reside, the Designs Registry will accept a statement of novelty that is calculated to place emphasis on the portion or portions having the novel shape. Whereas such a statement undoubtedly prompts the court to attach greater importance to the portion for which novelty is claimed than if novelty had been claimed for the design as a whole, the other portions of the shape will by no means be ignored completely. The tendency will still be to give consideration to the novel part in relation to and in combination with the old or common parts. As one judge appropriately remarked when it was pleaded that all the common features should be disregarded in determining validity and infringement, 'All human faces have two eyes, a nose and a mouth. People are not recognized by excluding these common features from one's mind.'

Wherever possible, therefore, the novel part should be made the sole subject of a registration so that it can later be considered by itself. If the novel part is not made and sold separately, the best course is to direct attention to its shape in the statement of novelty even though the latter is not necessarily decisive in determining the scope of protection afforded by the design registration. Thus, in a counterclaim for infringement brought in a threats action (unlawful threats are discussed in chapter 5 of this book), the judge found that sideboards had been copied by taking the glass and back from one registered design and adding to it a feature taken from another registered design. He held that there was no infringement because the sideboards, *taken as a whole*, were different from any one of the registered designs. The judge said: 'It appears to me that if it is desired to protect a particular feature in the general design of a sideboard it must be registered or claimed separately.'

Despite the advice given above, one can be too clever in seeking broad protection for part of the shape of an article. An applicant once attempted to obtain two registrations for one and the same design of a window stay, the applications having statements claiming novelty for respectively different parts of the shape of the window stay. The Hearing Officer held that this amounted to an attempt at obtaining two registrations for the same design or separate protection for parts of an article that were not made and sold separately. The shape of an article must be judged as a whole and cannot be subdivided. This should be distinguished from separate registrations for the shape and pattern of the same article, where the shape is regarded as one design and the pattern as a different design. The applicant could have filed a single application in which emphasis to the parts in question is given by colouring one of them red and the other blue and claiming that novelty resides in the shape of the part coloured red and in the shape of the part coloured blue. The Appeal Tribunal endorsed the Hearing Officer's views. By reason of this decision, the Designs Registry nowadays also refuses one application for the shape of a whole article and a second application for the shape of part of the same article, because the part is already protected in the first application and a second registration would be tantamount to obtaining duplicate protection for the part.

2.9 Set of articles

A design is registrable in a single application for a set of articles specified in the application form. To qualify as a set, all the articles must be of the same general character, they must ordinarily be on sale or intended to be used together, and each must have applied to it either the same design or the same design with modifications or variations which are not sufficient to alter the character or substantially to affect the identity of the design. Each article of a set must, of course, also meet the requirements of an article as explained in preceding sections. In fact, wherever this book refers to an article, the remarks are also applicable to any one article of a set.

The advantage of a single registration for a set of articles is that it is cheaper to obtain and maintain than several separate registrations in respect of all the pieces of the set; and yet the protection afforded by a set registration is by no means inferior; the registration will be infringed even if only one piece of the set is copied. A typical example of a set of articles is a coffee service for which the cups, saucers, plates, coffee pot, sugar bowl, and milk jug all bear the same new pattern, or a writing set comprising a fountain pen, propelling pencil, and ballpoint pen, sold together and having substantially the same novel shape, or a nest of tables. A coffee service of novel shape is not likely to constitute a set if it is only the shape which is new (as distinct from the pattern applied to it) because, say, the saucer shape is vastly different from that of the milk jug even though some characteristic may be common to both of them and to the other parts of the coffee service, that is to say even though all the parts may be based on a common theme. Type used by printers falls into the same category; although a common trait or style may be recognizable, each letter of the alphabet is necessarily different and in a case decided on a different point, the Appeal Tribunal expressed doubt that a fount of type constitutes a set of articles.

The Registrar's decision on whether a number of articles constitutes a set is absolutely final, there being no possibility of appeal. This is not often a hardship because it is cheaper to file separate design applications than it would be to prosecute an appeal if such were permissible. Indeed, a single application in respect of only one article of the various items making up the set may for practical purposes be quite adequate. A competitor who is prevented, by fear of design infringement, from making a tea cup bearing a particular pattern, is unlikely to make and sell only the saucers and/or plates; he is effectively prevented from competing in the whole line.

2.10 Eye-appeal

Reverting to the meaning of a registrable design as given in section 2.1, it is a stipulation that any or each of the four design features of shape, configuration, pattern and ornament exhibited by the finished article should appeal to and be judged solely by the eye. It cannot be over-emphasized that this is not the same as saying that the finished article must give pleasure to the beholder. After all, tastes differ; that which appeals to one person may be less attractive and even repulsive to another. For commercial reasons, a design should, of course, be pleasing to most people so that the article offered to the customer has sales appeal but this is a matter of taste and, like artistic merit, is not a prerequisite for registration. What is meant here is that the design of a finished article should call attention to or attract the eye—be perceivable or recognizable by the eye but not necessarily possess visual qualities to which every eye will take a liking. Putting it another way, appearance is all that matters in a registrable design. The design need not possess aesthetic or artistic appeal; it is sufficient if the features are capable of being appreciated so as to make an impact on the eye. But if the design was developed for a machine component that is hidden from view during normal use, it will be most difficult to prove that it possesses eye-appealing features in addition to the features which make it useful and efficient.

Thus, functional attributes of an article that do not call attention to the eye and cannot be appraised by the eye are disregarded, as was the case with an electric terminal which had been developed solely to meet the practical requirements of a washing machine manufacturer. Similarly, normally invisible internal features of a finished article, such as a pump housing, watch case, electric iron and carpet sweeper, are generally excluded from protection by the registration procedure; so are designs that are too minute to be discernible with the naked eye, although for small designs that are still noticeable (details of an intricate brooch) the Designs Registry will accept, and indeed call for, a magnified illustration.

The eye to which a registrable design should appeal and by which it should be judged is not that of a court or a design expert but the eye of the customer because it is the customer who finally selects or rejects an article for its appearance and, if there is nothing in the appearance that might influence a customer's choice, the design simply does not merit protection under the design law, although it might do so under some other law. There must be some addition to or embellishment of the basic form required by the article.

Eye-appeal is so fundamental a consideration in design law that it is interesting to observe in this respect how design law tends to change as new court decisions are handed down, thereby affecting the practical advice that clients are given from time to time. In a 1931 High Court case concerning the alleged infringement of a golf ball design, the judge commented as follows on the words 'appeal to and are judged solely by the eye' as used in the definition of a design:

> Now there is, I think, no possible doubt that 'the eye' in that section means the eye of the court, because the court has

ultimately to determine these questions, and it is the eye of the court and the eye of the court alone which has to be the judge of the design in question. That I think is plain from the language of the section, and it is made even plainer by the authorities to which I have been referred. The eye is the eye of the court, but the court is entitled to be assisted and instructed by evidence so that when it applies its eye to the test, it may have a mind to direct its eye which is instructed by the proper evidence. Such instruction may certainly be given to the court by persons who are competent to do it with regard to the prior art; that is to say, the court is entitled to be told what the designs earlier than the registered design represent, the differences or similarities between the earlier designs and the registered design and the alleged infringing design. Evidence of that sort to instruct the court is clearly relevant, and the court must clearly pay attention to it.

This tenet, that the eye is that of the court, was followed in several subsequent cases coming to trial but, despite the 'no possible doubt' referred to, was in effect unanimously overruled by the House of Lords hearing an appeal in 1971. Lord Reid then stated explicitly:

Those who wish to purchase an article for use are often influenced in their choice not only by practical efficiency but by appearance. Common experience shows that not all are influenced in the same way. Some look for artistic merit. Some are attracted by a design which is strange or bizarre. Many simply choose the article which catches their eye. Whatever the reason may be, one article with a particular design may sell better than one without it; then it is profitable to use the design. As much thought, time and expense may have been incurred in finding a design which will increase sales. . . .
Then there come the words 'Being features which in the finished article appeal to and are judged solely by the eye'. This must be intended to be a limitation of the foregoing generality. The eye must be the eye of the customer if I am right in holding that the policy of the Act was to preserve to the owner of the design the commercial value resulting from customers preferring the appearance of articles which have the design to that of those which do not have it. So the design must be one which appeals to the eye of some customers. And the words 'judged solely by the eye' must be intended to exclude cases where a customer might choose an article of that

shape not because of its appearance but because he thought that the shape made it more useful to him.'

Other Law Lords hearing the 1971 action concurred, using the words: 'The eye concerned will be the eye, not of the Court, but of the person who may be deciding whether or not to acquire the finished article possessing the feature in question', and 'I agree that the eye in question is the eye of the customer on a visual test'. Since the House of Lords is the highest court in the land, its decision supersedes the earlier High Court ruling. From that day on, therefore, an interpretation of the law that had been accepted unquestioningly for at least 40 years was upset at the stroke of a pen and everyone has had to adapt to the new meaning. There can be no better example demonstrating the advisability of seeking professional help on problems affecting design protection because no layman can hope to keep up to date with the ever changing interpretations. (Eye-appeal is also discussed in sections 2.21 and 5.20.)

Finally, it might be stressed in connection with 'eye-appeal' that there should be either the object or the result of making an appeal to the eye. The law, as has been shown, is not exclusively concerned with the author's intention at the time he conceived his design. He may have set out to develop a strictly functional article with all its features carefully selected to serve a mechanical purpose but, if the resulting design nevertheless possesses visual appeal to the customer, his design registration will be valid.

2.11 Excluded designs

To recapitulate, a design is excluded from registration if it has not yet been thought of when embodied in an article, if it is not capable of being applied to an article industrially, if it is applied to an excluded article, and if it does not, or is not intended to, appeal to the customer's eye. Old designs cannot be registered either (see section 2.19). There are still further grounds for a design registration being refused or being declared invalid and these will now be enumerated.

2.12 Method of construction

The Act stipulates that a registrable design should not include a method or principle of construction. This is understandable, bearing in mind that a design is concerned only with appearance, not how the appearance came about. The statement of novelty accompanying a design application must therefore not be so worded that it attempts to claim a general mode of manufacture that might result in other than the illustrated ornament or shape. One cannot, for example, claim a wickerwork basket when woven in a particular manner; it is the shape or pattern given to the basket that must be named. The Act does not, however, seek to exclude designs that can be executed by only one specific method or principle of construction. The position was very clearly described over 60 years ago by Lord Parker:

> A Design to be registrable under the Act must be some conception or suggestion as to shape, configuration, pattern, or ornament. It must be capable of being applied to an article in such a way that the article, to which it has been applied, will show to the eye the particular shape, configuration, pattern, or ornament, the conception or suggestion of which constitutes the Design. In general, any application for registration must be accompanied by a representation of the Design; that is, something in the nature of a drawing or tracing, by means of which the conception or suggestion constituting the Design may be imparted to others. In fact, persons looking at the drawing ought to be able to form a mental picture of the shape, configuration, pattern, or ornament of the article to which the Design has been applied. A conception or suggestion as to a mode or principle of construction, though in some sense a Design, is not registrable under the Act. Inasmuch, however, as the mode or principle of construction of an article may affect its shape or configuration, the conception of such a mode or principle of construction may well lead to a conception as to the shape or configuration of the completed article, and a conception so arrived at may, if it be sufficiently definite, be registered under the Act. The difficulty arises where the conception, thus arrived at, is not a definite conception as to shape or configuration, but only a conception as to some general characteristic of shape or configuration, necessitated by the mode or principle of construction, the definite shape or configuration being, consistently with such mode or principle of construction, capable of variation within wide limits. To allow the registration of a conception of such general characteristics of shape or configuration might well be equivalent to

allowing the registration of a conception relating to the mode
or principle of construction. Thus, in *Moody v. Tree* (9 R.P.C.
333) the Design registered was a picture of a basket, the claim
being for the pattern of the basket, consisting of the osiers
being worked in singly and all the butt ends being outwards.
Obviously, there could be made by this method of construction
any number of baskets differing in pattern, except that all
would have a certain common characteristic due to the method
of construction and visible to the eye. It was held that the
registration was bad, as being an attempt to register a conception as to the mode of construction, and not as to shape,
configuration, pattern or ornament. Similarly in Bayer's
Design (24 R.P.C. 65), the Design registered was a picture of a
corset, the novelty claimed being that it had the gores or
gussets cut horizontally from front to back. It was held that this
was not a Design capable of registration, being a conception as
to method of construction only, although all corsets made by
this method would have in common a peculiarity due to that
method, and visible to the eye.

Attention has been drawn to an apparent loophole in this aspect of
the law. If a manufacturer applied for protection of several designs
in a corresponding number of applications, each application being
directed to a different or modified shape for the same article
without detracting from its desired function, the resulting series of
registrations could conceivably control all possible ways of making
that article and hence the registrations might together effectively
protect a method or principle of construction although none of
them does so alone. Such an attempt to prevent others from
competing can, however, fail for other reasons, particularly on the
grounds of lack of eye-appeal and functional considerations.

2.13 Functional designs

Features of shape and configuration 'dictated' (in the sense of
caused or prompted) solely by the function that the article possessing those features has to perform are also excluded from registration. The emphasis here is on the word solely. Design features may
by all means be functional; indeed, in a majority of cases they are,
but they must also be provided for the purpose of eye-appeal. By
way of example, a pressure bar for a mangle or wringer was
declared to be validly registered and in fact the registration was

held to be infringed by someone who made something similar. One test that has been applied in court is the consideration of whether or not the intended function of the article so impeded the freedom of design that the manufacturer had no option but to adopt the shape that was sought to be protected. The classical decided case in this respect involved an electric fuse, shaped as a rod with bevelled collars intermediate the ends so that it would fit into a holder on a particular machine. By reason of this strictly functional aspect, the registration was declared invalid even though the fuse shape was conceived before the machine had been developed.

In the past, it has often been argued that, since most shapes can be altered without affecting the intended function of the articles having those shapes, the danger of invalidity on solely functional grounds must surely be remote. This argument has been held unsound in a House of Lords case (the same case as that referred to in section 2.10 in connection with eye-appeal) concerning an electric terminal for a washing machine, one of the Lords commenting as follows:

> It was argued on behalf of AMP [the appellant] that as there could be variations of shape in terminals that would success-fully do what was required of them then the features of shape would not have been dictated solely by the function which the terminals would have to perform. In my view, this contention is not sound. If there are alternative features of shape but if each one is dictated solely by the function which is to be performed by the article then each one would be excluded from the expression 'design'.

The criterion is whether a particular shape was conceived for, and actually serves, only a functional purpose. If so, protection by a design registration is impossible. The situation is not saved by the fact that other shapes can be called to mind for fulfilling the same function because these other shapes are, again, being thought of for functional reasons alone. In the electric terminal case the designer set out to make an article that would do the job. No feature of shape was provided for a purpose other than function and the registration was invalid. There was no 'blend of industrial efficiency with visual appeal' and it was admitted that the terminals would be bought for their performance, delivery and price and not for appearance. The fact that the article was normally hidden from the user's view of course confirmed the contention that it was not designed for eye-appeal.

The shapes of slotted angles, brackets, channels and similar constructional elements, buckles, fasteners for clothing, motors, window latches, wall plugs and countless other functional articles have been accepted for registration at some time or other but it must not be assumed that all these registrations are bad. For example, the operative end of a key is dictated solely by function but its other end is not; it can and does receive a variety of shapes without detracting from its function of a handle and these handle shapes are chosen to attract the customer. Similarly, although a slotted angle for supporting shelf brackets may be primarily designed to serve a mechanical purpose, its final shape will usually also be governed by appearance—not purely functional considerations.

A few other examples of decided cases may help to clarify the point. In a design registration for a spring clip, the statement of novelty claimed a part circled in red, which was a thumb groove at the end of the clip. The design was distinguished by this thumb groove from an earlier registration which used a dimple instead. The judge commented that in his opinion the groove served only a functional purpose and the change from a dimple to a thumb groove amounts to no more than an ordinary trade variation.

In the hot-water bottle action referred to in section 2.3, where the design had the striking characteristic of parallel diagonal ribbing over the front and back, the defendants' attack on the validity of the registration was also based on the arguments that the design included a method or principle of construction and that it included features dictated solely by function. This attack failed because, first, the use of a two-part moulding technique for making the bottles was not affected by the design registration, which did not seek to protect every conceivable surface configuration of ribbing, and, second, although the ribbing might have been provided for the purpose of better heat radiation without burning the user, the choice of the distinctive diagonal ribbing was not affected by this desired function. In any case, there was no evidence that the desired effect required the use of ribs in preference to other moulded projections. The registration was declared valid and infringed, at the trial and again on appeal. A member of the Court of Appeal remarked 'I think that the fact that it is functionally useful may be taken as established, but I am not satisfied for myself that the defendants proved that it was that object, and that object alone, which dictated the adoption of this type of ribbing.'

The striking novelty in the registered design of a windscreen for motor cycles resided in a vertical channel or bulge provided to lend strength to the windscreen, which was made from thin transparent plastics sheet. It was established that the outline shape of the windscreen was generally old but that previous windscreens did not require the strengthening channel because they were made from thicker inherently stiff material. The judge held that, since the channel, which was a common expedient for strengthening articles, was provided for purely functional purposes, it should be disregarded. The design registration was consequently declared invalid.

The examiners at the Designs Registry frequently raise the objection that the features of the design applied for appear to be purely functional and such that they would be judged by the purchaser only on their performance for the intended purpose, rather than their appearance. If the applicant cannot truthfully reply that the design was developed with a view to appealing to the eye of prospective purchasers, or the nature of the article is not such that a purchaser can really be expected to prefer one article to another by reason of its aesthetic appeal, the chances of obtaining a registration are slim.

2.14 Illegal or immoral

The Registrar can refuse to register a design if its use would, in his opinion, be contrary to law or morality. It will be noted that it is the Registrar's opinion that is material here, so he is given the powers of a censor whose attitude may or may not be a liberal one and could change with the times. He will supposedly consider a design immoral because he finds it to be obscene, indecent or sacrilegious, for example a pornographic photograph on a wallet or a portrait of a famous person on a toilet seat. An illegal design might be one in respect of electrical equipment that happens to be banned in this country because it is unsafe. To the author's knowledge, the Registrar's discretion has not in this respect been exercised against an applicant but one cannot be certain that the provision has never been applied since refused applications are not published. One imagines that the Registrar will be guided by decisions under similar provisions in the copyright law where, in one case, even a comical publication about Adolf Hitler was considered to be in bad taste or vulgar in the year 1939 and therefore undeserving of copyright protection.

2.15   Portraits

A design including the name or portrait of a living or recently deceased person, particularly royalty, may require consent from that person or his personal representative, or a registration could be refused. The same applies to armorial bearings, insignia, orders of chivalry, decorations and flags. Figure 2.1 and certain comments quoted in section 2.23 in relation to that figure have a bearing on this subject.

2.16   Words, letters, numerals

There are a few occasions, such as in patterns applied to wallpaper, when words, letters, or numerals, might form the essence of a design. In all other cases, and this rule of practice is strictly enforced by the Designs Registry, they must be omitted or removed from the illustrations of the design as filed at the Designs Registry. Where they are essential to the design, the Registrar may insist on insertion of a disclaimer of any right to exclusive use of the words, etc. Numerals on a clock dial are not of the essence of a design; nor are wavelength numbers on a radio panel or dates on a perpetual calendar, as distinct from letters worked into a design for jewellery or lace.

2.17   Printing type

Printing type is a special case of a novel letter forming the essence of a registrable design but, as in all other cases, the design must be applied to an article—in this case not a set of articles, because a fount of type probably does not constitute a set of articles for inclusion in a single registration, as has been explained in section 2.9. Type faces or matrices can be registered individually, for what such registrations may be worth. A type is a three-dimensional piece of metal or wood having on its upper surface a letter, numeral, or other character for use in printing. True, the shape of the character will probably predominate in the overall design and be the decisive factor when determining novelty and infringement. However, the character on the type face is necessarily reversed in relation to the printed version and this could give rise to difficulties in infringement considerations unless the court is prepared to compare the prints. In fact, the Registrar makes it a practice to call not only for representations of type matrices in the form to be sold but also imprints of the type cast from the matrices so as to facilitate a comparison with other designs.

A registration for a three-dimensional type or matrix does not, of course, afford protection against reproduction of the novel character by methods that do not require the use of printing type. In essence, it is the design of the type that is protected—not the method of reproducing the novel character. Consequently, the registered proprietor is faced with a formidable problem in enforcing his type design. Another disadvantage is that, to be on the safe side, a separate design application would need to be filed for several of the types comprised in the fount or series to give some semblance of protection. Under the Copyright Act (discussed in chapter 7) a type face enjoys automatic copyright protection.

In one reported case of which the author is aware, the court held in the year 1916 that a design registration for a fount of printing type consisting of 76 letters, numerals and symbols can be infringed only if all 76 characters are reproduced in their entirety and in the same way as shown in the registration, infringement being avoided by changing the order of the letters. However, it was also held that the original drawings which were made before the letters could be engraved in reverse on a steel die were the subject of artistic copyright, and so were specimen sheets containing words and letters illustrating the type faces for the fount of printing type and these would be infringed by the making of matrices for casting the type.

An international agreement has been signed by which the member countries will introduce protection for type faces by a special national deposit (filing) system or within the framework of their existing legislation for industrial designs or artistic copyright. In the UK, it has been suggested that the copyright law be suitably amended to include more positive protection for type faces. It may be, however, that the Design Copyright Act 1968 (see chapter 7) makes a further amendment unnecessary.

2.18 Variable shapes

Articles of clothing are registrable subject matter if illustrated when laid out in the flat and fully extended condition. It is only in this manner that the shape of clothing is fairly constant. On a tailor's dummy or other form, an article of clothing possesses an assumed shape, i.e., a shape that depends on the form, while in use the shape would vary from one wearer to another. This rule of practice is not strictly followed. The author knows of at least two registrations for wig foundations in the form of galloons that were illustrated on model heads.

It has been established that designs applied to flexible articles such as bendable dolls, which can be manipulated to different shapes, can form the subject of valid design registrations. However, it is questionable whether this is so for articles having a shape that is never wholly definite. One can think of a peculiarly shaped toy balloon that happens to be impossible to lay out flat to a tolerably constant shape when in a deflated condition and where the final shape is also indefinite because it depends on the degree of inflation.

An application for the design of a necklace consisting of a multitude of floral units linked by bars (as was known for necklaces) was once refused by the Designs Registry because there was nothing distinctive about the oval shape in which the necklace was laid out whereas the appearance of the individual floral units was known from buttons sold by a well known group of chain stores. The Appeal Tribunal agreed with this decision.

2.19   Novelty

The principal requirement for registration is that an application should be for a new or original design. There has been more litigation on this than any other aspect. The wording is amplified in the Act by a statement explaining what the design should not be, namely not a design that has already been published or registered in the UK in respect of the same or any other article, nor a design which differs from a previous design in only immaterial details or in features that are variants commonly used in the trade. The meaning of many of these words will now be considered. A fundamental point to note is that the novelty of a design is determined by comparing it with prior designs even if it can be shown that these prior designs were unknown to the applicant for registration at the time his design was evolved.

2.20   New or original

It has been suggested by one judge that 'new' refers to a design that is different from anything that has gone before, while 'original' means an old form of decoration given to a registrable article for the first time. This interpretation is a logical one. Thus, bearing in mind the words 'in respect of the same or any other article' (section 2.19), a salt shaker made in the shape of a miniature beer bottle would be unregistrable if that shape was already known for a beer bottle. On the other hand, on the first occasion that the known shape of a Christmas tree might be applied to a salt shaker, the design is likely to be registrable because it will be recalled that 'article' is defined as any article of manufacture. Whereas a beer bottle is such an article of manufacture, a Christmas tree is not.

The best-known decided case on this subject concerns the ornamental design for a spoon handle representing a particular view of Wesminster Abbey as taken from a photograph. The design was held to be validly registered at the end of the last century when the law was different, but the result could very well be the same today. The fact that the design was taken from a photograph was deemed irrelevant. Originality was not denied to the design simply because the underlying idea of representing public buildings on spoon handles was old. Nor was originality destroyed by the design having been taken from a source well known and freely available to the public, because a building is not an article of manufacture. Consequently, there was originality in first applying this particular view of Westminster Abbey to a spoon handle. Of course, a trade rival could not have been prevented from using a view of St Paul's Cathedral on his spoons or, for that matter, a different view of Westminster Abbey; what was protected was the view as registered, or colourable imitations of it that the eye judges to be the same.

Although a design is registrable only if it is applied to the article by industrial means, a new manner of industrial application does not necessarily impart novelty or originality to the resulting design. Where a lace design is applied by a new combination of movements of the lace-making machine, the design is not saved from anticipation if there are known designs of similar appearance, even though different movements were involved in applying the known designs.

2.21 Degree of novelty

As to the amount of novelty to be possessed by a registrable design, the rule discussed in section 2.10 still holds good: the eye is the only judge. This is why, as compared with patents for invention, it is more difficult to determine whether a design is anticipated by a previous design or, indeed, whether it infringes a previous design. One person's eyes rarely convey the same impression as those of another, even if both persons look at the design objectively.

To quote one learned judge in an action where a design for coffin plates was held to be old by the trial judge in the High Court but new by the Court of Appeal 'This, of course, is a question on which opinions may differ'. This is probably stating the obvious, but the reader is invited to consider the implications. When a designer first seeks professional advice on how best to protect his design, the design agent may be of the opinion that a design registration will afford good protection because he considers the design to be new, despite the existence of some prior design of which the designer is aware. The next person to express an opinion may be the examiner, and possibly the supervising examiner if there is doubt. The question may then go to a Hearing Officer, whose opinion possibly differs, or to the Appeal Tribunal, which might be the first to agree with the original opinion offered to the designer. Even if a registration is then granted, the High Court may express a different opinion again during the course of infringement proceedings; still other sources of differing opinions are the plaintiff's and defendant's barristers and various witnesses, the Court of Appeal and the House of Lords.

What makes things even more difficult at times is the uncertainty of the law. From whose point of view are designs compared for novelty? In section 2.10 it was mentioned that, until the House of Lords held otherwise in 1971, it was generally believed that the eye to which a design must appeal in order to be registrable is the eye of the court. Since the House of Lords judgment, the Court of Appeal has commented, but not actually ruled, that the consumer's or customer's eye is probably also decisive in comparing a registered design with an allegedly infringing design. If this is so, then there can be little doubt that it must also be a customer's eye which decides whether a design is new over a previous design.

The following guidelines are available for assistance in assessing novelty. Stated simply, a design is novel over a prior design if it exhibits pronounced differences, even though it may have been inspired by the prior design. 'There are very few designs which are entirely new. . . . They are made up from the old'. This was expressed by a judge very many years ago.

2.22 Immaterial details

Novelty is not imparted by immaterial details. A few embellishments here and there, replacement of an occasional straight line by a curve, the addition or omission of a minor ornamental feature, and changing the size (without materially changing the proportions) can all be trivial variations in relation to the design as a whole. In connection with dimensions, a Lord Justice of the Court of Appeal once said 'I unhesitatingly say that there is nothing new or original in taking that which has been done in landaus and proposing to do it on the smaller scale suitable to perambulators.' Even a change in proportions might not result in a different design. In an infringement action, where the design was to be applied to a servant's cap and consisted of the shape of a heart with a rosette resting on each lobe of the heart, the judge held that there was no infringement by a cap which had very much larger rosettes in relation to the size of the heart but he added that an infringer should not necessarily be allowed to get off simply because he has taken different proportions. The appearance as a whole must be different to avoid infringement. It so happened that in this case the registered design was not new anyway.

A good test is to determine whether the overall appearance of the article to which the allegedly new design has been applied is different. If the finding is in the affirmative, it is reasonably safe to conclude that the differences are substantial. It should not, however, be overlooked that the design may be novel though some, most or even all of the parts of the design are old when considered by themselves; it is the overall effect of the combination that must be new for the design to be registrable. An example quoted in an old court case mentioned a jockey shown on one button and a horse shown on a second button; were a third button to have the jockey of the first button mounted on the horse of the second button, a new combination results. The following is an example of where a combination of features failed to bring about a new design. A design for a toy bouncing horse was refused registration by the Designs Registry. The horse had its forelegs and hindlegs extended and looked the same as in a previous design registration owned by the applicant, except that there were bar rests instead of stirrups. The supporting structure for the horse was markedly different from the prior registration and altered the identity of the design, so that association of the designs (section 2.34) could not be entertained. On the other hand, the supporting structure was not new; an almost identical structure was shown in a periodical but for a horse in a different attitude. The Appeal Tribunal agreed that there was no substantial novelty in combining the two old features, that it was an obvious variant to replace the horse in the periodical with the galloping horse of the prior registration, and that there was no identity with the design of the prior registration to permit association.

Practically the same considerations arose, with the same results, in an application by the same applicants for a folding chair having one of its arms shaped as a table, the folding chair having been the subject of a previous registration and table arms for non-folding chairs being known from prior publications.

It will be recognized that the adaptation of an old design by taking only a part of it can conceivably also lead to a new and registrable design. A shade for an electric lamp was considered by the Court of Appeal to lack novelty because it looked just like a shade for a gas lamp, except that the now useless chimney required for gas lamps had been omitted; the old shade had merely been adapted to electric lighting and the overall appearance was still the same. It was stressed, however, that this did not necessarily mean that the omission of something from an old shape could never result in a new or original shape.

An applicant sought to register a design for a box having a base to serve as a playing board with holes for receiving pegs, the holes being arranged for the game of 'Chinese Checkers'. The Designs Registry cited a similar box in which the holes were arranged to be suitable for playing Solitaire. The Appeal Tribunal agreed that the design applied for was not novel or original. It is probable that the application could also have been rejected on the previously discussed ground that the differences in appearance were dictated solely by function.

2.23   Trade variants

It is also laid down (section 2.19) that a design is unregistrable if the only differences from prior designs reside in features that are variants commonly used in the trade. Put another way, the introduction of commonly used trade variants to an old design cannot make it new or original and registration will be refused, other than in exceptional circumstances referred to later.

If a particular shape is known for a fruit bowl and someone were to adapt it for a lamp shade, he would have to invert the shape and provide a hole in the surface that used to be the base of the bowl. If the resulting adaptation is not already barred from registration by the fact that the feature of the extra hole is dictated only by the function that the lamp shade has to perform, it would almost certainly be rejected as a common trade variant because it is conventional practice—common trade knowledge or a common matter of taste or choice—to have a top opening in a lamp shade to permit it to be supported on a lamp socket. A better example might be a case that has actually been quoted in court. If it was usual trade practice to provide some running shoes with spikes, then the addition of spikes to a particular running shoe that had a known shape but had not previously been made with spikes could not result in a new or original design. At the beginning of the century, there was a court action in which another judge pronounced a registration invalid on much the same grounds, although the judgment was expressed in different terms. The reason given was the 'common knowledge' of twisting a tube so as to convey gas around a corner, the design being for a gas jet consisting of a gas pipe bent to run round the entrance of a baker's oven. Today, the design would also be thrown out on functional considerations.

It is of no avail to argue that a design is not materially different from some previously published design except in a feature or features constituting a commonly used trade variant, if only one or two publications or prior registrations are available to show that an article of the same description has previously exhibited this alleged trade variant. The emphasis is on 'commonly' and 'used'—not merely occasionally or only published in print. 'Commonly used' requires evidence that the variant has been available from more than just one origin and, what is more, available in the UK. A single trade catalogue is certainly not sufficient to show that a feature is a common trade variant. To judge the issue, evidence will usually be necessary from an expert, an instructed person who knows common trade usage in the UK in the class of articles to which the design is pertinent.

Figure 2.1 illustrates the representations of a design application that had been refused by the Designs Registry. The design consisted of a coin for a pendant, the coin having two arcuate, together almost circular, cut-out portions framing Her Majesty's portrait. The view of the Designs Registry was that the design, being the same as the design of an old halfpenny, was not new or original since it is common practice in the jewellery trade to use obsolete coins as pendants or as parts of items of jewellery, and it is also common practice to use cut-outs. The Appeal Tribunal did not accept that cut-outs are a commonly used trade variant, nor that there is no substantial difference between the design of the application and a halfpenny, so that the appeal succeeded. The following, albeit disjointed, quotations from the Tribunal's judgment are

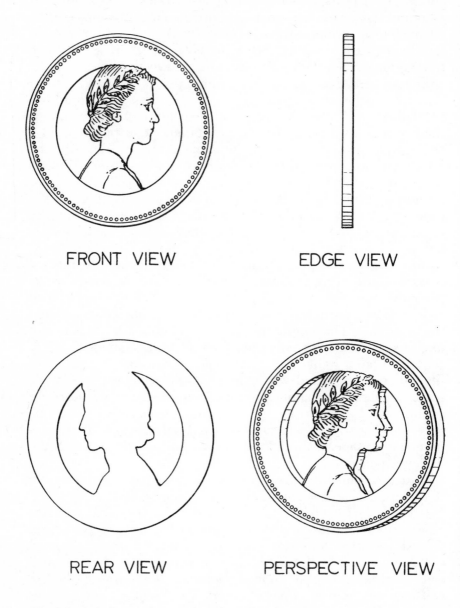

FRONT VIEW   EDGE VIEW

REAR VIEW   PERSPECTIVE VIEW

Fig. 2.1 Coin for pendant; registration refused by Registry, allowed on appeal

illuminating because they touch on several interesting aspects of design law and give the reader an indication of how thoroughly every detail is considered by the judge:

One has only to look at the representation of the design to see at the outset that it bears a close resemblance to a coin of the realm. It is not really very easy to ascertain from the representation of the design precisely what coin it might represent . . . . The possibility of other objections forms no part of the decision appealed against. It is, however, fair to say, having regard to the provisions of the Designs Rules, to which I was referred, and in particular Rule 24, which provides that if a portrait of any member of the Royal Family is to form part of the design, the Registrar need not proceed with the registration unless a consent is obtained, that in fact the applicant in this case appears to have secured a consent to registration from the Lord Chamberlain's office which I understand would be acceptable to the Registrar. The applicant has also taken the trouble to approach the Treasury with a view to seeing whether there might be any possible offences against the Coinage Acts, and the Treasury have given an indication that in their view the use of obsolete halfpennies for this purpose, punched out in this way, would not constitute an offence against any of the provisions of the Coinage Acts, and would be a use to which the Treasury would have no objection . . .

In the decision what is said is that it must be accepted that so far as the jewellery trade in general is concerned it is a common enough practice to use coins or articles of this character as pendants or as part of items of jewellery and this much is accepted by the applicant for registration. It is also suggested in the decision in the Office that cut-outs are a common practice in relation to articles of jewellery in the form of a disc. While the applicant is prepared to accept that there may in fact be known instances of cut-outs in articles of this general character in the form of a disc, he is not prepared to accept it is in any way usual in relation to discs which bear a central figure or head to cut out the surrounding portion so that the central figure remains, as it were, silhouetted in the centre of the disc, and in the absence of any evidence that this is a common practice, although it appears to have been accepted at the Registry as being a common practice, I do not think I am entitled to proceed upon the basis that it is in fact a common practice, and I do not propose so to do . . .

Although the Office wrote a letter, which was read to me, which indicated initially that they were proposing to object upon the basis that the cutting out of portions in the manner shown in the application for registration was nothing more than a common trade variant, in the end the decision I think really turns upon the basis that there is no substantial difference between the design sought to be registered and the halfpenny as such.

The decision itself refers to certain authorities which are very well known, which draw attention to the fact that if a design is to be registered at all there must be substantial novelty and that it is certainly not enough to produce something which differs from what has gone before only to some very slight extent and in a very trivial way, and in this connection one must always bear in mind the observations which have been made in past cases relating to registered designs, on which I think I need only quote the words of Bowen, L. J., in *Le May v. Welch* (1885) 28 Ch. D 24 at 34, in a case relating to the design of a collar: 'It is not every mere difference of cut, every change of outline, every change of length, or breadth, or configuration, in a simple and most familiar article of dress like this, which constitutes novelty of design. To hold that would be to paralyse industry and to make the Patents, Designs and Trades Marks Act a trap to catch honest traders.' If one applies the test 'a trap to catch honest traders', what I think his lordship was pointing out here is that if the difference is a very trivial difference, one which some other honest trader would be likely enough to happen upon without ever a sight of the registered design in question, being in no way a change of any materiality whatsoever, it would be wrong by reason of the registration to stop others producing similar articles.

In truth I think in this case it is very difficult indeed to say that the design applied for is not substantially different from a halfpenny. I do not think anybody looking at the design, although they might think there was a connection between the design and a halfpenny if they bore the appearance of a halfpenny in mind, would ever for one moment think it was a similar article. The cut-out itself I think produces a very strikingly different effect overall in the appearance of the article . . .

It is conceded in the decision appealed from that it is the practice of the office not to refuse a registration if there exists at the date of the application for registration some reasonable doubt as to the registrability of the design. If there is a reasonable doubt as to the registrability it is the practice in the Office to resolve such doubt in favour of an applicant. I am by no means sure that in this case I would not myself go further, but I think for present purposes it is sufficient for me to say that I think there is a very real doubt as to whether or not it might ultimately be held that this design as applied for is new and original as against a halfpenny as such, and accordingly it is my view that the appeal before me should be allowed.

As already mentioned, a novel design might result from a new combination of old features, and the remark also applies to a new combination of commonly used trade variants.

2.24 Anticipations

We now turn to the subject of exactly when a previous design is a bar to registration. A design is anticipated, i.e., not new or original and therefore not registrable, if it has already been published or registered in the UK (section 2.19). The patent rules and case law appertaining to the anticipation of inventions have been applied to designs by the courts, so for a complete study one would have to investigate the decisions under patent law and determine to what extent they are appropriate to designs. It is not the author's intention to do so in full, although an indication will be given of the considerations involved.

Publication, which means making available to the public, includes not only descriptions in printed form but also use, offer for sale and actual sale—virtually any action resulting in disclosure of the design to outsiders, other than in confidence. Further, 'publication' does not necessarily mean making available to all or most of the public. To invalidate a registration or show that a design is unregistrable it is enough to prove that the design in question was freely accessible to the public or disclosed to a single member of the public without any express or implied obligation of confidence. On the other hand, a widely circulated document expressly labelled 'Confidential' has also been held to be published (because of the wide circulation). It does not matter how ancient a prior design that proves damaging to novelty might be because, in contrast with patent law in the UK, under design law publications more than 50 years old are not excluded as citations against a design.

The crucial day on which the design still has to be novel is the date of filing the application for registration in the UK or, in the case of a Convention application (chapter 3), the priority date that is being claimed. The time of day is unimportant. If a design is being published at 9.00 today, it suffices if the application for registration is filed by, say, 17.00 today (but care should be taken that the application reaches the Designs Registry during office hours).

It is repeated that it is immaterial whether or not the design applicant or proprietor knew of a damaging prior publication—it is just as damaging if it has for many years lain forgotten on a shelf.

2.25   Prior printed publication

This bar to the validity of a design registration is more or less self-explanatory. If substantially the same design has previously been publicly described or illustrated in print (printing includes other forms of reproduction and multiplication such as photography, xerography and stencil copying), the subsequently filed design application will be refused by the examiner if he happens to be aware of the anticipation or finds it during his novelty search. Alternatively, any registration that is granted despite the existence of a prior printed publication in this country will be invalid (but see the exception mentioned in section 2.33).   The earlier document must clearly disclose substantially the same design, or the same design modified by a commonly used trade variant or immaterial details. To anticipate a design, it is not possible to make a mosaic of two or more prior printed publications because, as already indicated in sections 2.22 and 2.23, a design could be novel as a result of combining several features which are known *per se*, provided that the combination has not been suggested before. Examples of prior printed publications are English or foreign books, magazines, advertisements, trade catalogues, newspapers and leaflets that are, or were at the material time, freely accessible to the public in the UK. Only one copy of the publication in a public library or in a private library to which the public has access would suffice to render a design unprotectable by registration. There is no need for proof that someone saw or read the publication; its availability in the UK is enough.

The striking eye-appealing feature of a toy bucket that once came into dispute was a Maltese Cross impressed in the base so that the bucket appeared to rest on four short legs and, when used at the beach to make a sandcastle, would produce four turrets on top of the castle. A secondary feature was that the circular handle had the appearance of a rope. The design registration was attacked on three grounds: (a) function, (b) method or principle of construction and (c) novelty. The Court of Appeal rejected the first of these grounds because the argument failed to take the striking castellated exterior shape of the article into account, which played no strictly essential part in the function of shaping sandcastles. The second objection was supported by the argument that the shape in question was the most economical and satisfactory for moulding the buckets from plastics material. This was also rejected, not simply because the design registration was not restricted to plastics buckets but mainly because it was held that the words 'method or principle of construction' as used in the Act had the effect of excluding a process or operation by which a shape is produced, as opposed to the shape itself, which did not apply in this case. Third, on novelty, the main citation was a patent specification which described, *inter alia*, a two-part sandcastle mould with a battlemented top. There was considerable doubt that the various words used in the patent specification could be construed to mean a sand bucket precisely of the kind illustrated in the design registration but, said the Appeal Court, even if they did, the description in the patent specification did not constitute a publication of the design because there was no illustration which could be compared with the registered design by the eye alone, or a description that could be seen by 'the mind's eye'. The patent specification did not even relate to a bucket with a handle.

2.26 Other prior publications

Imparting non-confidential knowledge of a design other than in printed form could be by way of exhibitions in the UK (but see section 2.30), displays in showcases, showrooms and museums, the disclosure of a design to prospective customers with a view to soliciting orders, and prior public use in the UK. The latter includes actual sales and all instances where the design has already been industrially applied to an article and that article is not kept secret or confidential.

2.27 Prior registration

A UK design registration of prior date is also damaging to the novelty of a later design that is not materially different. This is so, irrespective of the sequence in which the designs were registered, that is to say, regardless of which registration was the first to be laid open to public inspection and have its certificate of registration issued.

Consider the case where similar designs are the subject of two applications by different proprietors. The application with the earlier filing date or priority date (see Convention applications, discussed in chapter 3) takes precedence of the later application and will prevent the later application from being registered. This is because a design is registered as of the filing or priority date. The Designs Registry endeavours to ensure that of two conflicting applications pending simultaneously, the one with the earlier filing or priority date is examined and dealt with first but it sometimes happens that the registration certificate on the later application issues first; in that event the registration granted on the later application will be invalid. For example, the situation can arise where someone in this country files design application A and obtains a registration on it as of the UK filing date of 1 February. Later, say on 1 June, a Convention application B for the same subject matter is filed in this country claiming priority from a foreign application that was filed on 1 January. The result will be that registration B renders registration A invalid by reason of prior registration, even though A was the first to be filed in the UK and the first to mature into a registration, because B is registered as of the priority date 1 January whereas A is registered as of 1 February.

2.28   Exempt anticipations

Certain acts of prior publication, prior use, and prior registration are specifically excluded as grounds for refusing subsequently filed design applications or for invalidating their registrations. These will now be discussed one by one. Attention is also directed to section 3.14, which deals with Convention applications; the very purpose of such applications is to enable the proprietor to claim priority from his foreign filing date instead of having to rely on the later UK filing date, and therefore any intervening publication, use or registration is without effect.

2.29   Confidential disclosure

Information imparted to another person in confidence cannot result in refusal or invalidation of a subsequent design registration, no matter who made the confidential disclosure. In practice, it is often difficult to establish when something is disclosed in confidence. If the proprietor of a design reveals it to a toolmaker who is commissioned to make a mould for his exclusive use, it is likely that the toolmaker is under an obligation of confidence and any disclosure of the design by him to third parties will be in breach of confidence and therefore not a ground for invalidating a subsequently filed design registration obtained by the proprietor. However, if the proprietor shows his design to several prospective customers to test the market before he incurs the tooling costs and before he files a design application, it is more likely that there is no confidential relationship and that disclosure of the design will be a bar to obtaining a valid registration at a later date. A design that was shown to a friend to obtain his expert advice as to whether it would suit the market was once held to constitute a confidential disclosure that was not damaging to the novelty of a subsequently filed design application, notwithstanding the fact that the friend was a potential customer. It was said that the confidential relationship would have ceased as soon as the friend had placed an order for the articles.

For textile articles, the acceptance of 'a first and confidential order' is explicitly excused by the Act but the relationship of confidentiality is not explained except by reference to circumstances that would make it contrary to good faith for the recipient of the information to use or publish the design. It is always unwise to rely on the confidential disclosure exclusion. The design application should, if at all possible, be filed first and disclosed afterwards. Where this is not possible, the proprietor should, to avoid all doubt, ask for written confirmation that the design is being shown in strict confidence (also see section 8.3).

2.30 Certified exhibitions

A newly designed product is often unveiled at a trade fair or other exhibition, the exhibitor deciding only at a later date whether or not to seek design protection by way of registration, depending on the reception that his product has received. Design law permits a delayed design application under such circumstances, provided that the exhibition has been certified by the Department of Trade and Industry and provided also that the design application is lodged within six months of the opening date of the exhibition. What is here excused is (a) the act of displaying the design at the exhibition by the proprietor, or with the proprietor's consent, and consequential publication of a representation of the design, and (b) display of the design during and after the exhibition without the proprietor's consent.

This concession is not restricted to exhibitions registered at the International Exhibitions Bureau under the 1928 International Convention relating to International Exhibitions. Any certified exhibition qualifies but the Department of Trade and Industry obviously cannot automatically certify every exhibition that is held in the UK. An exhibitor is therefore well advised to take the initiative if it is likely that he might wish to avail himself of the exempting provision under the Act. He goes about this by writing before, or at the latest during, the exhibition to the Industrial Property Department of the DTI located at the Patent Office, stating the full official title of the exhibition, fair or show, its commencement and closing dates, its location, the organizer's name and address, and the kinds of articles being exhibited. These particulars should be accompanied by a request that the exhibition be certified in accordance with Section 6(2) of the Registered Designs Act 1949.

It is important to note that a certified exhibition saves only a subsequently filed *British* design registration from invalidity. Publication or use of the design at the exhibition can very well jeopardize the chances of obtaining valid corresponding protection abroad because not all foreign countries have similar provisions for excusing disclosures at shows. Note also that, after the exhibition has closed, sales by the proprietor of articles bearing the design are not excused. Further, it is only consequential publications of the design that cannot be used to invalidate a subsequently filed design application.

An application for a chair design was once refused registration by reason of the publication of illustrations in the periodical *The Cabinet Maker and Complete House Furnisher* issued a single day before the design application had been filed. It was argued that this prior publication should be excused because the illustrations in question showed articles to be exhibited at the Furniture Show 1957, which had been certified by the then Board of Trade. However, the Designs Registry held that the publication could not be regarded as being in consequence of the exhibition because it occurred five days before the exhibition had opened. It is interesting to speculate whether the applicant for registration could have succeeded on the far better argument based on copyright (see section 2.33).

2.31 Disclosure to government

Communication of a design by the proprietor to a government department or to a person authorized by a government department to consider the merits of the design, and anything done in consequence of such communication, is likewise excused as a prior publication or prior use. One must not be under the misapprehension that this proviso is an exemption for all kinds of disclosure to a governmental authority. It covers only cases where a design or the article bearing the design needs, say, government approval or testing. Care should also be taken in determining what constitutes a government department; many national organizations are nowadays set up by authority of the government but are autonomous and do not constitute actual departments.

2.32 Experimental use

Prior use by way of industrially applying a design to articles prevents a valid registration from being obtained subsequently only if the articles were not kept secret or confidential. Accordingly, where prototypes are made industrially, this does not constitute harmful prior use if the prototypes are intended for experimentation and reasonable precautions are taken to keep them from public view.

2.33 Prior use of artistic work

Another situation where a design registration is saved from invalidity or the application is not refused by reason of prior use applies to designs corresponding to artistic works.

It is laid down that, where copyright subsists in an artistic work and an application for the registration of a corresponding design is lodged by or with the consent of the copyright owner, such a design shall not be treated as old by reason only of any previous use made of the artistic work, unless such previous use was made by or with the consent of the copyright owner and involved the marketing of articles embodying an industrial application of the design (or a substantially similar design). In a reported case where this provision was considered, a carpet sweeper had been made and used abroad and an illustration of this foreign product had even been published in a foreign periodical which was freely available in the UK; but the product had not yet been made and marketed in the UK. It was held that a subsequently filed UK design application was not detrimentally affected by the earlier publication relating to the foreign use of the industrial design. Although this was not made clear in the decision, presumably the magazine illustration was considered to be the artistic work to which the design of the British application corresponded; alternatively, the artistic work was a set of working drawings for the sweeper, but these drawings were not produced.

Following this decision, the practice of the Designs Registry has been to permit registration of a design which was previously illustrated in a locally available foreign periodical, provided that the applicant files a statutory declaration to substantiate the facts on which he relies. The important circumstances to be declared are, of course, that the design corresponds to the artistic work shown in or represented by the prior publication, that the applicant for registration is the owner of the copyright in the artistic work or had the copyright owner's permission to file the British design application, and that there had been no previous use of the design in the UK in so far that there had been no authorized previous local marketing of articles to which the design (or a similar design) had been applied industrially. It will also have to be established when the copyright in the artistic work expires because the term of the design registration can in this case be no longer than for the artistic copyright.

2.34   Associated designs

The previously described exempted anticipations have all related to certain acts of prior disclosure by publication or use of the design. There is, finally, an exceptional provision for enabling so-called 'associated' designs to be registered after prior UK registrations for similar designs have already been granted in respect of the same or different articles.

Let us assume that a proprietor owns a registration for a pistol design to be applied to a firearm. At any time while this registration is still in force, the same proprietor may seek a supplementary registration for the same pistol design in respect of another article, say a cigarette lighter, irrespective of whether the design had already been published or used when applied to a firearm. Also, the proprietor may seek a supplementary registration in respect of the same article (the firearm) or another article (the cigarette lighter or a toy or a charm for a bracelet, etc.) of a design that consists of the previously registered pistol design with changes not sufficient to alter the character or substantially to affect the identity of the design, again irrespective of any prior publication that may have been made of the original design. Supplementary registrations of the type just described can be regarded in somewhat the same light as patents of addition for improved or modified inventions under the patent law. The reader may therefore find it easier to understand the significance of an associated design if it is stated that improvements in or modifications of a previously registered design, or the application of a previously registered design to a new article, can be protected by the innovator in a subsequent registration, which then has a kind of 'design of addition' status. The term of protection of the associated registration is limited to that of the parent registration. If the parent registration is not renewed or is declared invalid, the associated registration also ceases.

It should be observed that an associated design registration is restricted to the case where one and the same proprietor owns the parent design and has applied for the associated design or where he becomes the registered proprietor of the parent design before the associated design is registered. Thus, if someone files an ordinary design application and the official search reveals that a very similar design has already been registered by another person and is still in force, the applicant must first purchase the earlier registration before his application can proceed for an associated design.

An associated registration for a modified design is likely to afford only limited protection because the proprietor, by accepting association, is virtually admitting that such changes as have been effected are not sufficient to alter the character or identity of the parent design. Nevertheless, it is advisable to obtain an associated design registration on the principle that two registrations are better than only one. The second registration could possibly catch an infringer in circumstances where the first registration fails to do so. If an applicant files two similar design applications on the same day, association is not required unless they claim different priority dates (this refers to Convention applications that are discussed later).

3. *Application for registration*

3.1 How to file an application

The design registration procedure, as distinct from design law, in the UK is not a complex one and can be readily understood by the layman. Briefly, what is involved is the filing of an application on the prescribed form accompanied by the requisite number of illustrations or samples and, in most cases, a statement of novelty. The application then receives a number, is officially examined for novelty and registrability and to see if all formalities have been met and, if everything goes well or any official objections can be overcome, proceeds to registration. Of course, a government fee is also payable on filing but this is not unduly high and covers registration for the first five years. The design registration number is the same as the application number and this is of great assistance to a manufacturer who may not wish to wait until after registration to incorporate the number in a mould or on a label. He can simply refer to 'Design No . . .' in the knowledge that the number will not change, but obviously he must not use the word 'registered' until the registration certificate has actually been issued.

In order to provide the reader with a realistic example of the application procedure in the UK, the author devised a design of his own and obtained a registration for it. The documents for the registration are illustrated in Figs. 3.1 to 3.7, starting with a page from the designer's sketch book and finishing with the official registration certificate. These documents will be referred to under their appropriate headings.

For ready reference, the following is a check list of the information required prior to filing the application for registration.

(a) Name, address and nationality of the applicant(s).

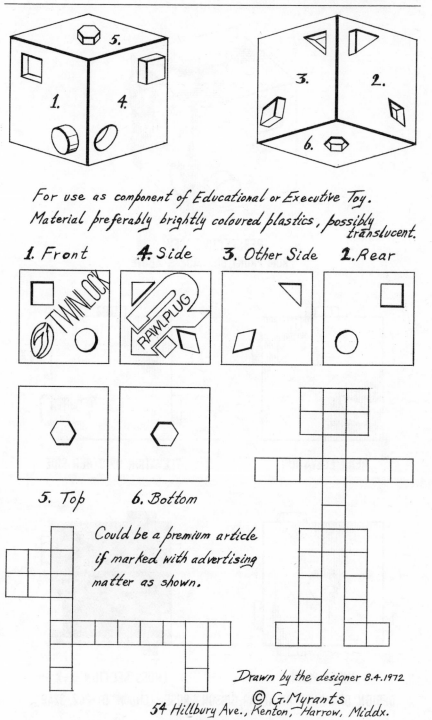

For use as component of Educational or Executive Toy.
Material preferably brightly coloured plastics, possibly translucent.

1. Front   **4.** Side   **3.** Other Side   **2.** Rear

5. Top   **6.** Bottom

Could be a premium article
if marked with advertising
matter as shown.

Drawn by the designer 8.4.1972
© G. Myrants
54 Hillbury Ave., Kenton, Harrow, Middx.

Fig. 3.1   Page from a designer's sketch book

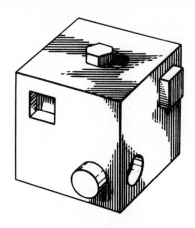

**PERSPECTIVE VIEW
FROM FRONT, ONE SIDE & ABOVE**

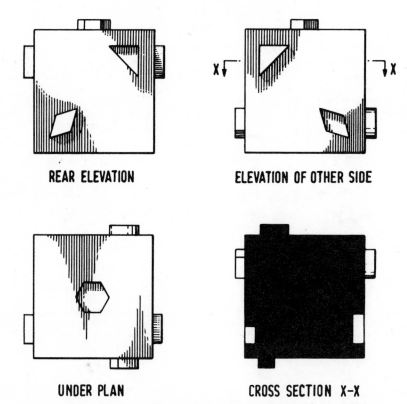

REAR ELEVATION   **ELEVATION OF OTHER SIDE**

UNDER PLAN   **CROSS SECTION X–X**
DESIGN DRAWINGS BY ALGAR, GIBSON & ROSE. LONDON 01–242 3240

Fig. 3.2   Formal drawings for a design application

Form Designs No. 1

REGISTERED DESIGNS ACT, 1949

Authorisation of Agent

(*a*) Here insert name
and address of agent.

I (or We) have appointed (*a*) TRADE MARK CONSULTANTS CO.

of 54 Hillbury Avenue, Harrow, Middlesex, HA3 8EW

(*b*) Here state the
particular purpose for
which the agent is
appointed.

to act as my (or our) agent for (*b*) all my design matters

and request that all notices, requisitions and communications relating thereto may be sent to such agent at the above address. I (or We) revoke all
previous authorisations, if any.

(*c*) Here state nation-
ality.

I (or We) hereby declare that I am (or we are) a (*c*)

British subject

(*d*) To be signed by
the person appointing
the agent; if a body
corporate, a director
or the secretary should
sign.

(*d*)

Address 54 Hillbury Avenue,

Harrow,

Middlesex, HA3 8EW

Dated this 13th day of April, 19 72

To the Registrar,
  Designs Registry, The Patent Office,
  25 Southampton Buildings,
  London WC2A 1AY

or (optionally, in the case of Textile Articles only) *at*
  Designs Registry, Manchester Branch,
  Baskerville House, Browncross Street,
  New Bailey Street, SALFORD M3 5FU

4950/699s. D.185238 10M 7/70 T.P. Gp.658

(SEE OVER)

Fig. 3.3 Authorization of agent to represent applicant (obverse side)

Extract from Rule 2 of the Designs Rules, 1949

"Agent" means an agent duly authorised to the satisfaction of the Registrar.

Rule 8 of the Designs Rules, 1949

(1) Every applicant in any proceedings to which these Rules relate, and every person registered as proprietor of, or as having an interest in, a registered design, shall furnish to the Registrar in addition to his full residential or business address an address for service in the United Kingdom.

(2) Such address may be treated, for all purposes connected with such proceedings or design, as the actual address of such applicant or person and shall, in the case of a registered proprietor, be entered on the register as the address for service of such proprietor.

(3) Any written communication addressed to an applicant in any proceedings, or to any person registered as proprietor of, or as having an interest in, a registered design, at his address for service shall be deemed to be properly addressed.

Extract from Rule 10 of the Designs Rules, 1949

(1) An application for registration and all other communications between an applicant and the Registrar, and between the registered proprietor of a design and the Registrar, or any other person, may be made by or through an agent.

(2) Any such applicant, registered proprietor or other person may appoint an agent to represent him in any proceeding or matter by signing and lodging with the Registrar an authority in writing to that effect on Form Designs No. 1, or in such other form as the Registrar may deem sufficient.

(3) In case of such appointment, service upon the agent of any document relating to the proceeding or matter shall be deemed to be service upon the person so appointing him, and all communications directed to be made to such person in respect of such proceeding or matter may be addressed to such agent and all attendances upon the Registrar relating thereto may be made by or through such agent.

Fig 3.3   Authorization of agent to represent applicant (reverse side)

THIS BOX FOR OFFICIAL USE

Form Designs—No. 2

FEE: ITEM 1

REGISTERED DESIGNS ACT, 1949

Application for Registration of Design
(except for Textile articles)

(a) Here insert (in full) the name, nationality, and address of the applicant or applicants.

Application is hereby made for registration of the accompanying design in the name of *(a)* GEORGE MYRANTS,

a British subject,

of 54 Hillbury Avenue,

Harrow, Middlesex, HA3 8EW

who claim(s) to be the proprietor(s) thereof.

(b) Here state the article to which the design is to be applied as shown in the representations.

The design is to be applied to a *(b)* toy constructional unit

(c) (d) Strike out one or both paragraphs, if inapplicable.

(c) The design has been previously registered for one or more other articles under No.

(d) The design consists of the design previously registered under No. with modifications or variations not sufficient to alter the character, or substantially to affect the identity thereof.

My (or Our) address for service in the United Kingdom is c/o Trade Mark Consultants Co., 54 Hillbury Avenue, Harrow, Middlesex, HA3 8EW.

(e) Signature.

(e) *Trade Mark Consultants Co.*

Dated this 13th day of April, 1972

TO THE REGISTRAR,
DESIGNS REGISTRY, THE PATENT OFFICE,
25 SOUTHAMPTON BUILDINGS,
LONDON, WC2A 1AY.

N.B.—THREE identical representations or specimens of the design should accompany this Form, and except in the case of an application in respect of wallpaper or lace, it should further be accompanied by a statement of the features of the design for which novelty is claimed.

(C784702)   Dd. 185735   12m   6/72

Fig. 3.4   Application form

TRADE MARK CONSULTANTS CO.
International Trade Mark and Design Agents

54 HILLBURY AVENUE   KENTON   HARROW   MIDDLESEX   ENGLAND
Telephone: 01-907 6066   Cables: Lexique Harrow

The Registrar,   Our ref: GM/JSB

Designs Registry.   13th April, 1972

Dear Sir,

On behalf of GEORGE MYRANTS, the applicant for registration of the design,
we state that the novelty resides in the shape and configuration of the
article as shown in the representations.

Yours faithfully,

Trade Mark Consultants Co.

Lexique Ltd.; Directors: R. MYRANTS, G. MYRANTS, Dip.E.E., A.R.M.T.C., M.S.E., Grad. I.E.Aust., F.I.L.

Fig. 3.5   Statement of novelty

Ack. No. 3

THE DESIGNS REGISTRY,
THE PATENT OFFICE,
25 SOUTHAMPTON BUILDINGS,
LONDON, WC2A 1AY.

George Myrants.

956961

ref 9M/JSB

The Registrar acknowledges the receipt this day
of your application to register a design, which will
receive attention in due course.

The application has been numbered as above,
and this number should be quoted in any further
communication relating to the application.

N.B.—This Card is *not* a Certificate of Registra-
ion of the design.

6532 D.185387 5M 3/71 T.P. Gp.658

Fig. 3.6 Official filing receipt

UNITED KINGDOM OF GREAT BRITAIN AND NORTHERN IRELAND
AND THE ISLE OF MAN

D.R. No. 1

REGISTERED DESIGNS ACT, 1949

Certificate of Registration of Design

Number of Registration   956961

Date of Issue of Certificate   *24th* May 1972

This is to certify that, in pursuance of and subject to the provisions of the Registered Designs Act, 1949, the Design, of which a representation is annexed, has been registered in the name of George Myrants

as of the   13th   day of   April 1972

in respect of the application of such Design to a toy constructional unit.

EDWARD ARMITAGE
Registrar.

Subject to the provisions of the Act and Rules copyright in this Design will subsist for five years from the earlier above mentioned date, and may be extended for two further periods, each of five years.

Designs Registry,
The Patent Office,
25, Southampton Buildings,
London, WC2A 1AY

6467 D.185381 5M 2/71 T.P. Gp.658

956961

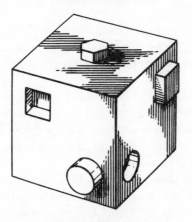

**PERSPECTIVE VIEW
FROM FRONT, ONE SIDE & ABOVE**

REAR ELEVATION

ELEVATION OF OTHER SIDE

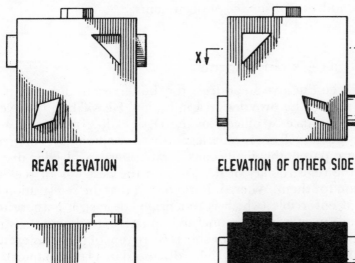

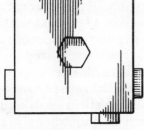

UNDER PLAN

CROSS SECTION X-X

Fig. 3.7 Certificate of registration

(b) For a Convention application, the country in which, and the official date on which, an identical design application was first filed abroad.

(c) For a Convention application to be filed by an applicant who was not the applicant abroad, the nature and date of, and parties to, the instrument by which the applicant acquired his rights.

(d) The design feature(s) to be named in the statement of novelty and any disclaimer or emphasis to be mentioned.

(e) The designation of the article to be specified in the application form and, in the case of a set, the trade description of each article comprised in the set.

(f) The number of any previous UK registration of the same design obtained by the same applicant but for another article.

(g) The number of any previous UK registration obtained by the same applicant in respect of a design of which the present design is a modification or variation that has not changed the character of the design.

(h) The correct application form to use.

(i) The address for service of documents.

3.2 Design registration agents

Anyone who can give an address for the service of documents in the UK may file his own design application. He will be given every possible assistance by officers of the Designs Registry in cases of difficulty but he will not receive legal advice or opinions from them. It will be apparent that many considerations are involved in deciding on the registrability of designs and the best way of seeking protection for them. Where it is important that the registration be valid and enforcible (which is practically always), it is therefore worthwhile to enlist professional assistance from a design registration agent, or design agent for short. By reason of the indifference with which designs and copyright (discussed in a later chapter), as compared with other forms of industrial property protection, are regarded in this country, few, if any, advisers have ventured to call themselves design agents. They are usually mainly engaged on other work. In the current climate, it would be a brave person who risks the establishment of a practice devoted solely to applying for design registrations on behalf of others and assisting clients in the enforcement of design registrations and artistic copyright.

Lists of persons or firms who profess to be design agents do not exist, so it is usual to consult a patent agent. Apart from solicitors, a patent agent is the only person who may, for gain, assist the owners of inventions in obtaining patents here and abroad and no one can call himself a patent agent without being registered. The many other services usually performed by patent agents in patent and other fields, including furnishing design and trade mark advice, can be, and often are, performed by unregistered persons. Thus, as trade marks have grown in importance and number, the profession of trade mark agent has developed and nowadays it is common for patent agents to leave trade mark work to trade mark agents. Design and copyright considerations, although in several respects closely related to patent questions, are often also delegated to trade mark agents and this is another reason why it has been difficult for a separate profession of design agent to grow up.

Design applications lodged and negotiated to registration by agents will necessarily cost more than if the applicant does the work himself—at least twice as much—but it is money well spent. If he is experienced, the agent will have useful information to make available to his client and in the long run an agent's expertise saves his client money. Foreign applicants for a UK registration are not compelled to use an agent but invariably do so because they must have a local address for service of documents and it is convenient to use the agent's address.

Figure 3.8 indicates at what stages during development and production it is desirable to consult a design agent. The figure necessarily covers subsequent stages in the protection and enforcement of design rights and copyright which will be described in more detail later in this book.

There may be numerous reasons giving rise to a new or improved design. Some of these have been indicated in Fig. 3.8, others will readily occur to the reader. In any event, the idea will then be embodied in an article by the designer, who may be a full-time employee, a freelance, a consultant, or several of these persons. Representatives from the production department may also be involved in the developmental work. Whoever the developers might be and whatever the path followed, the tangible result of the work will be a sketch or a model and it is this that should be shown to the agent. The latter will advise whether an application for a design registration should be filed at this stage or later (preferably after a production sample is available) and what precautions are desirable to safeguard artistic copyright in the sketch

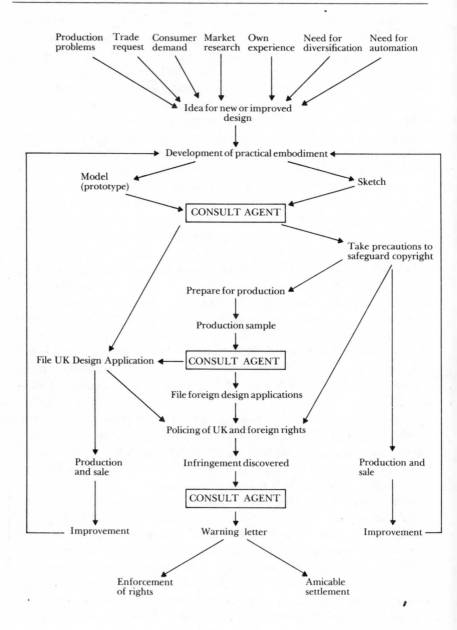

Fig. 3.8 Consulting a design agent

or model. Production and sale must not commence until after the UK design application has been filed. If there is an improvement in the design in the course of time, the agent should again be consulted with a model or sketch. Policing of the UK and foreign design rights and copyright is the task of the owner of the rights, possibly with the help of his customers, licensees, trade associations, etc. Whenever an infringement is discovered, the agent absolutely must be consulted before anything else is done; only with his advice can it be decided whether there is a cause of action and how an out-of-court settlement might be negotiated.

3.3 Application formalities

The application should be made in the name of the proprietor, be for a new or original design and specify the article or set of articles that the design is to be applied to. The representations to accompany each application may be photographs or drawings but in certain cases specimens can be filed or may be officially demanded. Documents should be on 13 inch × 8 inch paper having a 2 inch margin at the left-hand side, but A4 size paper is acceptable.

3.4 Where and when to file applications

Applications are normally filed at the Designs Registry in London, next to the Patent Office; the Registry opens at 10.00 and closes at 16.00 on all weekdays, except Saturdays and holidays but documents may be left at the Patent Office between 16.00 and 18.00 on weekdays. On Saturdays, new applications other than Convention applications may also be left at the Patent Office between 10.00 and 13.00. If desired, applications in respect of only textile articles may alternatively be lodged at the Manchester branch of the Designs Registry between 10.00 and 16.00 but the future of the Manchester branch is somewhat uncertain, there being rumours that it may be discontinued. If applications and other documents are lodged by post, the filing date is deemed to be the date of delivery in the ordinary course of the post. Papers lodged by hand after the above-mentioned times are deemed to have been filed on the next following business day. This is important to bear in mind; filing an application one day late can make all the difference to the validity of the resultant registration. No business is officially transacted on public holidays, bank holidays, Sundays and special days as may be announced.

It is interesting to note that, while special 'non-business' days, known as excluded days, are declared at times of national crises such as postal strikes, the classes of business that are excluded invariably fail to cover the filing of new ordinary design applications which do not claim Convention priority. This is understandable. While a foreign applicant in the UK can always prove that he filed a corresponding application in his home country on a particular date and it is therefore an easy matter to announce that he is permitted to file the British application on the first normal business day after the crisis that gave rise to the excluded days has passed, notwithstanding that more than six months may by then have expired, a locally resident applicant has no verifiable date to claim back to. He must get his application papers to the Designs Registry despite the national crisis or postpone exploitation of his design. In either case, therefore, he is at a considerable disadvantage as compared with the applicant who resides abroad. Luckily, national crises are infrequent.

3.5 Applicant

A design application has to be filed by the proprietor of the design. This is the author of the design or the person for whom the author executed the design for good and valuable consideration or the person in whom the design (or the right to apply the design to an article) becomes vested such as by assignment. A person who obtains the sole trading rights in articles to which the design is applied is not entitled to make the design application unless he has also acquired the manufacturing rights. If the proprietor dies before the design is registered, the particulars of the new owner may be substituted in the application provided the death and new ownership are adequately substantiated. A simple change of name of a company may also be effected while an application is still pending, a certificate being required from the Registrar of Companies or an equivalent document for a foreign company. A change in proprietorship involving an assignment after the application has been lodged must await recordal until after issue of the Certificate of Registration.

A person who has acquired a share in a design can apply for registration as joint proprietor but the individual rights possessed by co-proprietors are not regulated by the Designs Act as they are in patent law. Very often co-proprietors have disputes and then fight tooth and nail over how to dispose of the joint property. Difficulties also arise out of how to license a jointly owned registration if one of the parties is not in favour. To avoid these and other problems, the agreement whereby a person acquires a part-interest in a design should make adequate provisions for dealing with such eventualities. Certain licensees could also apply for registration, for example a person or company licensed to apply the design to a particular article, but it is usual for the design proprietor to be the applicant. The term 'licensee' must not be confused with a sales organization that simply holds the distribution or selling rights (franchise) for articles but takes no part in their manufacture.

3.6 Author

Disputes may arise as to who is the true author of a design. The author is the designer—the one who conceived or created the design in the first place and reduced it to a visible form, whether by drawing or making a prototype, even if the finishing touches were applied by someone more competent who was told to do so by the designer, or if minor modifications necessary for production purposes were suggested by, say, a mould maker. In one decided case, a rough sketch and verbal instructions from an employer to a workman, who produced a design from this information as intended by his employer, disentitled the workman to call himself the author. In another case, a person who made a sketch of a design to be applied to woven goods but who gave it to a weaver without specific instructions on how the design should be worked out was held not to be the author of the design. The weaver was the author because he was given considerable latitude; with the incomplete instructions given to him he could just as well have produced a cloth identical with a known prior design.

Note that the first UK importer of a foreign design is not entitled to obtain a UK registration in his own name without permission from the foreign owner because a person does not become an author by copying a design he has brought back from abroad. Under patent law, the first importer is regarded as the true and first inventor but there is no equivalent provision under the design law. The importer of a design must, preferably by way of an express assignment or licence, acquire a right in the design or a right for its application to an article before he can file a UK design application, the law and procedure being no different from those applicable to a design that was conceived in the UK.

A different situation is exemplified by the idea for a floral design for printing on textile piece goods that was submitted by a Persian trader to a British firm of calico printers whose designer translated the idea into a suitable practical working form, submitted the design to Persia for approval and then engraved it and had the design registered, whereupon the Persian trader placed orders. In infringement proceedings, it was alleged that the British firm was not the proprietor of the design but it was ruled that, even assuming that the Persian trader was the author of the design, the British firm had acquired the right in the design for good and valuable consideration and was therefore the proprietor.

3.7   Master and servant

If the author is employed or paid to execute a design for a principal, it is usually the principal who is the design proprietor and the rightful applicant for registration. The considerations then involve the law of master and servant. Employers and employees are in practice so often in doubt about their respective rights as affecting designs worked out during the course of an employment, that it is necessary at this stage to consider the various aspects in more detail, mainly with the help of reported cases on inventions under the patent law.

The duties and rights of an employee in respect of industrial property arise out of the contract with his employer as supplemented by any further implied terms.

3.8   Implied service contract

Dealing first with the more frequent case where, alas, there is no express service contract, a design made by an employee *in the course of his employment* is the property of the employer. If such an employee took out a design registration in his own name, he must hold the registration in trust for the benefit of the employer, even after termination of his employment.

The difficulty arises in determining whether a design was conceived in the course of his employment, i.e., whether it was part of the employee's job to do designing, and each case must be judged on its own merits. The fact that a design was worked out during the period of employment in the employer's time and with his materials or that the employer is using the design is not decisive. There is a contractual obligation on the part of the employee to exercise good faith. Sometimes this obligation is found in contracts, more often it is implied. The approach to be made is to inquire whether it is inconsistent with the good faith which ought properly to be inferred from the contract of service that the employee should hold the design for his own benefit. Use of the employer's time and materials could be a breach of contract but the penalty might only be damages—not necessarily forfeiture of the design registration. Unless there is an express provision in a contract, the employer is entitled to the design only if it would be a breach of good faith for the employee to retain it.

Thus, if someone is specifically employed to solve design problems or to do research, the results of his endeavours rightly belong to the employer, even if such results were obtained in the employee's own time. It would be contrary to good faith that the employee should hold the design against his employer. Except where a contract indicates otherwise, a draughtsman is, *prima facie*, employed to design; so is a chief designer and engineer. In fact, in a patent case where a chief designer was not asked to make a particular invention, the employer was nevertheless accorded the rights. A managing director or a general manager or a works manager would probably be in a fiduciary position towards his company, which is therefore the beneficial owner of the design.

3.9 Express service contract

Turning, now, to the case where there is an express service or employment contract, the foregoing considerations should not be necessary if the contract has been adequately prepared but care should be taken to exclude invalidating clauses from a contract. An express covenant on the employee's part not to use information gained in his employment has been held invalid as being in restraint of trade. The doctrine of restraint of trade rests on the principle that it is against public policy to prevent a man from employing his skill and knowledge unless it is reasonable for protecting his employer and it is not against public interest. Similarly, it is in restraint of trade to require an employee to assign designs which were made after termination of his employment. There is, however, no objection to requiring an employee to assign all designs relating to his employer's business and made during the period of employment, whether in the employer's time or not, because it is reasonable to require an employee to give his whole mind to his employer's problem. A requirement for the assignment of designs that are not remotely concerned with the employer's business could possibly be in restraint of trade and invalid.

3.10 Trade secrets

An employer may protect himself against disclosure of his trade secrets by the employee—both during and after employment—but if the clause in the agreement is too wide there is a danger that it is invalid as being in restraint of trade. Any restraint affecting the employee's rights in connection with the use of trade secrets after his service has ended should be drafted modestly so as to provide no more than adequate protection for the employer. Under common law, an employee is obliged to preserve secrecy regardless of whether or not there is a service contract, provided that he was told, or could reasonably be expected to assume, that certain information supplied to him is secret. The author is of the opinion that it is preferable to have a written contract which also regulates this aspect.

3.11 Draft contract

The following is an imaginary agreement drawn up between the author of this book and his company to regulate the question of trade secrets and the ownership of designs and copyright. This example is included only to give the reader an idea of what is involved. It should not be assumed that it contains the ideal wording and it would certainly be unwise to adapt the contract to meet different circumstances without obtaining legal advice.

THIS   AGREEMENT   is   made   this . . . . .day of . . . . .1976 between LEXIQUE LIMITED whose registered office is at . . . .(hereinafter referred to as 'LEXIQUE', which expression where the context so admits includes its successors and assignees) of the one. part and GEORGE MYRANTS of . . . . hereinafter referred to as 'the Designer') of the other part.

A. WHEREAS the Designer is employed by LEXIQUE in a confidential capacity and is also in a fiduciary position towards LEXIQUE by reason of being a director of LEXIQUE and therefore has been and will continue to be entrusted with trade secrets and other confidential knowledge.

B. AND WHEREAS it is the duty of the Designer to carry out and to assist in carrying out for the benefit of LEXIQUE research, design and other work on his own initiative or under the direction of a person appointed by the company or in his capacity as a director of LEXIQUE.

NOW IT IS AGREED as follows.

1. The Designer shall at all times during his employment and/or his appointment as director keep records, including notes, reports, sketches, plans and photographs of all work carried out in the course of his employment or directorship.

2. All such records and any documents of a secret or confidential nature provided by LEXIQUE shall be the property of LEXIQUE and shall be delivered by the designer to LEXIQUE on demand before or at the termination of the period of his employment or directorship.

3. The copyright in all such records shall at all times belong to LEXIQUE or its assignee and the Designer shall not without the permission of LEXIQUE retain any copies.

4. The Designer shall during the term of his employment and/or directorship promptly and fully disclose to LEXIQUE all work carried out in the course of his employment and directorship and all work carried out in any place and at any time during the said term utilizing any secret or confidential information which he has learnt or has himself discovered or evolved in the course of his employment or directorship.

5. Except as provided in clause 6, the whole right and interest in any design or artistic or literary work made by the Designer as a result of the work described in clause 4 shall be vested in LEXIQUE who shall be at liberty to decide what UK and foreign applications for design registration or provisions for other protection shall be made.

6. If any design or work of which the Designer is the author during the term of his employment or directorship is of no interest to LEXIQUE's present activities or those envisaged for the future, LEXIQUE shall give the Designer the opportunity to protect and exploit the design or work for his own benefit using his own time and resources.

7. The Designer shall, whenever requested to do so by LEXIQUE either during or after termination of his employment and/or directorship, sign applications, assignments or other instruments which LEXIQUE may reasonably deem necessary or advisable to apply for and obtain protection and for the purpose of

vesting in LEXIQUE or its assignee the whole right and title therein and LEXIQUE or its assignee is entitled to decide for what period any such protection shall be maintained at its expense.

8. The Designer shall not at any time except with the written consent of LEXIQUE either directly or indirectly use or divulge to any person not in the employment of LEXIQUE or its subsidiary companies any secret or confidential information which he may have acquired as the result of his employment or directorship but nothing in this agreement shall prevent the Designer from using any experience or skill or knowledge other than the abovementioned secret or confidential information.

9. LEXIQUE will not withhold consent to the publication through ordinary scientific channels or professional or trade associations of information relating to any design made by the Designer unless in the opinion of LEXIQUE such publication would adversely affect LEXIQUE's interests.

10. All previous agreements between the parties relating to the matters referred to in this agreement are hereby cancelled.

3.12 Consultancy agreements

It has been shown that the employer/employee relationship should preferably be regulated by a written employment contract because the conditions of employment are decisive in resolving the question of ownership of a design of which the employee is the author. When a freelance industrial designer or craftsman is commissioned to develop the designs of new products, or new designs for old products, a proper consultancy agreement drawn up by a solicitor is indispensable to leave no room for a subsequent dispute about the ownership of the design rights. A typical clause in such an agreement, where the freelance author has contracted to develop a design for a fee, might read as follows.

> I agree that .... Ltd shall have the sole and exclusive right in and to the design and in and to the artistic copyright, both in the UK and abroad, including the right to apply the design or any similar design to any article and the right to file British and foreign design applications and to claim priority for such foreign applications under the provisions of the International Convention and I hereby agree to sign all documents necessary or desirable to give full effect to this agreement.

3.13 Manufacturing agreements

Business establishments which develop designs and sell the articles but do not have their own producton facilities may likewise have a need for concluding an agreement with craftsmen, say with the tool or mould makers in whose factory the articles are manufactured and who possibly contribute to perfecting the basic design submitted to them. Again, it is advisable for a solicitor to draft a suitable document, but the following letter of agreement will give an indication of what is required.

> Unless we have come to a contrary arrangement in writing, in return for eventually placing orders for moulds or tools with you and also eventually placing with you orders for producing articles made with such moulds or tools when corresponding orders for articles have been received by us from respective customers, you agree that any contribution that you or your employees may have made to our ideas or the designs in which these ideas are embodied are our property to be protected in our name as we deem fit.

Without such an agreement, the most complex situations can arise. For example, a company of furniture retailers without manufacturing facilities of their own may give a self-employed carpenter instructions to make a particular kind of writing desk required to start a new line of office equipment. They might direct the carpenter as to how the desk is to be constructed, the kind of materials to be used and the precise design features it should possess. The order could be for one desk to start with to serve as a prototype, or even 100 desks to test the market, a price is agreed, and the carpenter is eventually paid on delivery. Everyone seems satisfied. Later, the new line proves to be a commercial success and a repeat order is to be placed but the carpenter now asks a price that seems prohibitive, so the furniture retailers look around for an alternative supplier. At this stage, the carpenter informs them that they must buy either from him or not at all because he has obtained a design registration to safeguard his rights. The retailers object violently on the grounds that the carpenter was originally commissioned to make a very particular desk according to their own specifications and was paid to execute the design, so the rights in the design must surely belong to them. The carpenter contends that he was paid only for supplying the original desk or desks, that the specifications he received did not regulate all the eye-appealing features of shape, that he is the author of the design and that he is therefore entitled to the design registration in his own name. A court of law may eventually find it possible to untangle the seemingly insoluble situation but how simple and cheap it would have been to regulate the position at the outset!

3.14   Convention applications

By an international agreement known as the International Convention for the Protection of Industrial Property, to which the UK is a signatory, a design application may be filed in the UK within six months of the first application for the same design in any other participating country if the applicant in the UK is the same as the applicant abroad or is his personal representative or assignee. If someone else filed the basic foreign application, the applicant in the UK is required to state the nature and date of the document by virtue of which he became the proprietor of the design and acquired the priority rights, but the document itself need not be filed.

The advantage of such a Convention application is that its effective filing date in the UK will be the foreign filing date (priority date) and the application cannot be refused by reason of any publication or use of the design that might have taken place here in the intervening period. Of course, similar rights and advantages are available to British designers who wish to apply for design registrations abroad, but there is one important exception. Foreign applicants in the UK may claim Convention priority from an 'International' design registration (discussed in chapter 6) whereas UK citizens are not even able to file 'International' applications, let alone claim priority from them in other countries.

New Convention countries are declared from time to time by Order in Council; an up-to-date list is available from the Designs Registry. In Figs 6.1 and 6.2, countries which were members of the Convention at the time of writing are indicated by a dagger. Most of the important countries have subscribed to the Convention.

The term of a UK registration granted on a Convention application is calculated from the priority date. Convention applications may be converted to ordinary applications, i.e., the claim to Convention priority may be abandoned during the application stage if the applicant provides the Registrar with an assurance that the design has not been published or used in the UK before the actual filing date in the UK.

3.15 Requirements for Convention applications

Convention applications absolutely must be filed within the stipulated six month period, no extension of time being obtainable. Only if the priority period expires on a Saturday, Sunday, holiday or excluded day may the application be filed on the next following business day. It is also essential that each Convention application be supported within three months of the UK filing date by an officially certified copy of the design representations or samples as filed abroad. This period is also not extensible—in fact it is the only time limit specified in the Designs Rules (as distinct from the Designs Act) which is excluded from the Registrar's discretionary powers to enlarge set times. If any part of the certified copy is in a language other than English, and this applies to foreign language documents in all other proceedings before the Designs Registry, a translation verified to the Registrar's satisfaction will be required. Translations verified by Fellows of the Institute of Linguists are acceptable to the Registrar without a statutory declaration.

Hardly any variation is permitted in a UK Convention application compared with the basic design as filed in the foreign country. For example, if the basic application was accompanied by an erected specimen of a collapsible display stand (it being common to file samples of all kinds in many foreign countries) then the British application must also be in respect of the erected display stand—not, say, a cardboard blank for the display stand. If the basic foreign application was filed with representations, the illustrations of the article in the UK representations need not actually be taken from the same viewpoints but no design feature may be added or omitted.

In other respects, Convention applications are treated in the same way as design applications of local origin.

3.16 Application form

Different application forms are prescribed to be filed to meet particular circumstances. The various forms are listed in Fig. 3.9 which also shows other important requirements (to be discussed later) that are peculiar to certain kinds of applications. Form 2 as used for non-Convention applications in respect of single non-textile articles is reproduced in Fig. 3.4. Applicants who employ an agent to do all the work for them need not concern themselves with any of these forms; instead, they lodge an authorization of agent on Form 1 (see Fig. 3.3). This may be worded to read as a general

List of forms and representations

A	B	C	D	E	F	G	H	J	K	L	M	N	P
Form No.	Form in duplicate	Single article	Set of articles	Non-textile Wallpaper	Non-textile Lace	Non-textile Other	Textile Checks & stripes	Textile Other	Priority claim under convention	Non-convention	Statement of novelty required	Number of representations or specimens 3	Number of representations or specimens 4
2		*		*						*		*	
2		*			*					*		*	
2		*				*				*	*	*	
3		*		*					*			*	
3		*			*				*			*	
3		*				*			*		*	*	
3	*	*					*		*				*
3	*	*						*	*				*
4			*		*					*			*
4			*			*				*	*		*
4	*		*				*			*			*
4	*		*					*		*			*
5		*			*				*				*
5		*				*			*		*		*
5	*	*					*		*				*
5	*	*						*	*				*
Manchester 1	*	*					*			*			*
Manchester 2	*	*					*			*			*

How to use this table
For an *applicant resident in the UK*, go down column L (ignoring column K) and select only that marked line which is also marked in column C and D and in one of columns E to J. Column A will then give the correct Form No., Column M indicates whether a statement of novelty is required, and the prescribed number of representations is read from either of columns N and P.

For a *non-resident wishing to claim priority* from his home application, the procedure is the same, but start in column K and ignore column L.

Fig. 3.9 List of forms and representations

authorization enabling the agent to file future applications without having to obtain the applicant's signature every time.

The applicant must state his full home or business address and an address in the UK for the service of documents. If he has a name such as Chu Man Fu or Robert John George, where it is impossible to distinguish the forenames from the surname, the latter should be underlined. A form lodged by a firm which is not recognized as an entity under the law in this country must contain the full names of all the responsible partners and be signed by all the partners or by one of the partners stating that he signs on behalf of the partnership or by any other person who can prove that he is authorized to sign. A document lodged by a body corporate has to be signed by the Company Secretary or a director or any other person who can satisfy the Registrar that he is authorized to sign;

this rule is the cause of the Designs Registry insisting that a statement of the signatory's capacity must appear adjacent to his signature—a requirement that has long been dropped for patent forms filed by companies.

3.17 Textile articles

A textile article is defined for the purpose of the Designs Act as meaning textile piece goods, handkerchiefs, shawls, elastic webs and any other article decided from time to time by the Registrar, namely a host of knitted and plastics piece goods set out in Fig. 3.10. It will be noted from Fig. 3.9 that special application forms are applicable to textile designs and that forms are required in duplicate (only one of these need be stamped with the government fee); also, a distinction is made between designs consisting principally of checks and stripes and other textile designs, the Registrar's decision being final in this respect.

At one time, the majority of design applications in the UK were in respect of textile articles. It is not necessary for the purpose of this book to ascertain the exact reason for this; a probable explanation is that the textile industry in this country used to be exceptionally strong and textile designs happen to lend themselves particularly well to protection by a registration procedure. It was not until after the Second World War that the percentage of textile design applications dropped to under 50 per cent. By 1950 the figure was over 50 per cent again. Since then, design applications for textile articles have dropped quite startlingly to under 10 per cent.

3.18 Separate application for each article

A registrable design has to be applied to 'an' article. Consequently, except in the case of an application for a design which is to be applied to a set of articles, a separate application is required for each article to which the same design is to be applied and for each article of a different design. Of course, each such application is also examined and otherwise treated quite independently except that the resultant registration may have to be associated with an earlier design, as is described in section 2.34.

There are some anomalies in how the 'separate applications' rule is applied by the Designs Registry. The contents of openable and reclosable containers need to be protected independently of the container and separately from each other. This is understandable.

Goods included in the official definition of 'textile article'

Elastic webs
Handkerchiefs
Knitted piece goods (not being lace)
Plastics piece goods (woven, netted or printed)
Shawls
Textile piece goods
Textile squares (to be made up into articles)

And the following, if made of textile material or from woven, netted or printed plastics piece goods

Altar cloths
Antimacassars
Bath mats
Bedspreads
Blankets
Braids
Cot covers
Perambulator covers
Counterpanes
Curtains
D'Oyleys
Duchesse mats
Face cloths and flannels
Kangas
Quilts (not being down quilts)
Rag books
Ribbons
Saries
Sarongs
Serviettes
Settee covers (not being loose covers)
Sideboard covers
Table centres
Table cloths
Table covers
Table runners
Tea cloths
Toilet covers and mats
Towels
Tray cloths
Trimmings

Fig. 3.10   List of textile goods

The articles inside a transparent disposable container, such as a bubble pack, which must be destroyed to obtain access to the articles, form part of the visible features of the design and must therefore be included in any application that is filed for the bubble pack. This is likewise understandable. On the other hand, a cruet set comprising a stand and salt and pepper shakers and a mustard pot loosely received in emplacements of the stand is, curiously, accepted as 'an article' in a single ordinary application—not an application for a set. One might think that an openable and reclosable container, say a canteen for cutlery, where the contents are deemed to be separate articles requiring separate applications, is distinguished from a cruet set because cutlery is often purchased piecemeal for placing in the same compartmented canteen whereas a cruet set is expected to be sold undivided. However, it is unlikely that this is the correct explanation because, in strange contrast, a toy train set comprising a locomotive and several carriages is required to form the subject of as many separate applications as there are components, even though the latter are intended to be sold and used together. Again, it is difficult to reconcile the above-mentioned rulings with the case of a single application allowed for a fastener for clothing, comprising no fewer than four component parts before assembly and two separate parts when assembled. The author has not infrequently been able to obtain single registrations for such fasteners of the hook and eye or press-stud type and the representations were even allowed to illustrate the parts before as well as after assembly. There is therefore no clear guideline that can be given as to what exactly constitutes an article for which a single design application will suffice. Nor is it surprising that the Designs Registry may receive applications which are mistakenly directed to more than one article. As will be explained later, the Registrar may then decide to permit the applicant to divide his application into several applications, each of which is the subject of a separate official fee and all of which are, exceptionally, deemed to have been filed on the original date, but such 'divisional' applications are suspect because there is no express provision for divisional applications under the Registered Designs Act. A single application covering the designs of several articles should therefore not be filed deliberately. If there is any doubt, a separate application should be lodged in respect of each article, accompanied by a letter explaining the circumstances and requesting deferment of examination and a refund of the official fee if a single application is acceptable.

3.19 Specification of article

The article or set of articles to which a design is to be applied must be specified in the application form and the terminology employed is important because it may make all the difference between winning or losing an infringement action. If the article is a fountain pen but the same design could also be applied to a ball point pen or propelling pencil, it is clearly safer to mention 'writing implement' (although the safest course of all would be to file three applications, each designated by the specific name of the article, or a single application for a set of articles). Where a generic term acceptable to the Designs Registry is chosen, the examiner may call for an additional copy of the representations for cross-searching purposes in the official files. If the design is for a clip that can be used for a variety of purposes ranging from a paper clip to a clothes peg, it will be wise to select the designation 'clip, primarily for use as a . . .' and then name the preferred use. Functional statements other than those expressed or implied by the name of the article should preferably be avoided so as to afford broader protection. For example, a design registration specified to be in respect of a collapsible vegetable rack might not be infringed by a similar design applied to a non-collapsible rack used for supporting or filing papers and it would therefore be preferable to specify no more than 'rack' or, if the Registrar so requests 'rack, primarily for use as a vegetable stand'.

In a case that has actually been decided, infringement of a design specified to be applicable to an 'audible alarm kettle' was avoided by a kettle which did not whistle. The kettle of the registration had distinct features of novelty in the shape of the body and the shape and location of the handle. The defendants' kettle was found to have substantially the same body and handle but differed markedly in the cap and spout. The trial judge said he felt unable to treat the registration as though it had been 'for a design applied just simply to kettles. If I could, that would plainly diminish the significance which is attached to the particular shaping of the audible alarm device'. Since the description of the article emphasized the audible alarm characteristic, the cap and spout responsible for that function had to assume a primary significance and the infringement action failed. The judge added:

> Let me make this perfectly plain, and it is only fair to the plaintiffs that I should say so. I fully recognize that the precise form of the design monopoly which has constrained me to

adopt the line of reasoning I have endeavoured to explain will not be known to the purchasing public to whom articles containing this registered design are primarily intended to be offered, so that it can be said, and said with a certain apparent justification, that the court may be adopting an unduly legalistic approach to what ought to be treated as a commercial matter. If that is thought to be a criticism requiring any consideration, there are two comments which might be made which would help to meet that. The first is that it was the registered proprietor himself who chose to confine his classification to goods in a restricted form and thus prevented this court from enlarging it and construing it as a registered design applied just for kettles *simpliciter*. The second is that, if a member of the public is seeking to choose an audible alarm kettle, it is practically inconceivable that the design features whereby the plaintiffs' type of audible alarm is differentiated from all others would in fact be overlooked. For those reasons, although I am satisfied that this is a validly registered design, I cannot hold that it has been infringed by the article admitted by the defendants to have been marketed by them.

In the case of a set of articles, the trade description of each article comprised in the set must be given in addition to the name of the set.

3.20 Statement of novelty

Not all applications need be accompanied by a statement of novelty. From Fig. 3.9 it can be seen that designs in respect of wallpaper, lace and all textile articles are exempt from this requirement. In view of its importance, it is difficult to understand why a statement of novelty should not be necessary for some articles and why it is not entered on the certificate of registration and in the Register of designs. It is simply open to public inspection and will be included only in a certificate prepared specifically for use in legal proceedings.

The statement should be typed on a sheet that does not contain other correspondence; no official form is provided for it. An example is shown in Fig. 3.5. The Registrar is also entitled to require the statement to be endorsed on each representation or specimen but this is a rare occurrence. Since it draws attention to features of the design that the applicant considers important or that he wishes to disclaim, the statement of novelty is akin to the claim in a patent specification, for which reason it is often also referred to as a statement of claim or a novelty claim.

The features of the design that can be claimed are four in number—shape, configuration, pattern, ornament—and have already been discussed. A typical statement of novelty might read: 'The novelty of the design resides in the shape, configuration, pattern and ornament of the article as shown in the representations.' Such a statement seeks protection for all the features in combination and is much the same as saying that the design should be considered as a whole because no one feature is deemed to be more important than another. However, if only the feature of pattern is claimed, the effect is to lay stress on that feature and disclaim the other features.

Careful thought should be given to selecting the best wording for the novelty claim, i.e., deciding which of the four features of novelty is or are to be mentioned, because it will be evident that the statement of novelty can affect the protection that will be afforded by the registration. Where there is no statement of novelty, such as for lace articles, the design is considered as a whole and it will not be an infringement for a competitor to take only a part of the registered design if the overall appearance of the competitor's design is different. When only pattern is mentioned, the judge in an infringement suit is likely to give little, if any, consideration to the shape, and vice versa. Thus, one of the judges in the Court of Appeal once said that a distinction between pattern and shape can be drawn by the applicant in the novelty statement if he likes. Where the applicant has limited his design to pattern, as was done in the case under consideration, then when considering novelty 'you are not entitled to go outside anything which fairly and properly falls within the definition of pattern . . . . You cannot find novelty in something which is clearly shape as distinguished from pattern'.

If more than one feature is mentioned, the features are considered in combination rather than separately. Where there is a claim for 'shape or pattern' or 'shape and, independently thereof, pattern', the two are unlikely to be considered independently of one another because at least one judge has commented that independent protection is obtainable only by means of separate registrations. Assuming, therefore, that novel features of shape and pattern are applied to a vase, the best course would be to file two separate applications, one illustrating the shape and pattern but claiming novelty in only the pattern and a second application illustrating the vase without the pattern and claiming novelty in the shape alone. The first of these two applications must not, however, be filed before the second as it will otherwise constitute a prior registration (section 2.27); both applications should be filed on the same day.

An unusual statement of novelty for a roulette wheel design was considered by the court in infringement proceedings. The statement said 'The novelty lies in the pattern applied to the rotor characterized by checkered sectors on the outer ring of the rotor of which the checks are the same width as the pockets, which checkered sectors are separated from one another by substantially smaller sectors of a colour different from those employed for the checkered sections.' The judge, not unexpectedly, commented that this wording robbed the illustrations of the design of any real value for ascertaining the design features and wholly misconceived the purpose of a statement of novelty. A statement of novelty is intended to direct special attention to the part of the illustrated design that introduces the proprietor's novel contribution.

If colour is essential to the design, the statement of novelty may read 'The feature of the design for which novelty is claimed is the pattern or ornament created by the tone or contrast of the colours applied to the article as shown in the representations.'

3.21 Disclaimers and other remarks in novelty statement

To summarize, one or more of the four registrable design features must be claimed in the statement of novelty. One alone has the same effect as disclaiming the other three. More than one, even if stated in the alternative, are considered in combination.

There are other remarks that may or must be included in the statement of novelty under certain circumstances. Should the representations as originally filed include an insufficient number of views and the subsequently filed views for the first time bring important features of the design to light, then these features will have to be disclaimed in the novelty statement because they are not entitled to the original filing date. A disclaimer of the kind just referred to might be expressed: 'The novelty of the design resides in the shape of the article, excluding the handle, as shown in the representations' or '. . . excluding the part marked A as shown in the attached representations'. The last-mentioned wording would require a marked copy of the representations to be attached to the statement of novelty.

Voluntary disclaimers are also possible and are inserted by applicants when they wish certain parts to be disregarded, although it is more usual in this case to stress the important features of shape by identifying them with a coloured wash or reference letter in an extra copy of the representations attached to the novelty statement, which would say: 'The novelty of the design resides in the shape of the parts of the article shown coloured blue in the attached representations.'

The following extracts are from the judgment in an infringement action and should be read in conjunction with Fig. 3.11:

> . . . the application bears an endorsement as to novelty in the following language: 'Novelty lies in the shape of the article having the ends coloured blue shaped as shown in the representation.' The representations which were attached show a side view, an oblique front view [see the redrawn upper illustration in Fig. 3.11, where the diagonally hatched parts were coloured blue in the original] and a front view, and do not specifically illustrate the back end or rear of the structure. . . . There is, as I see the matter, no real difficulty in construing the protection afforded by this registration. . . .
>
> I entertain no doubt whatever that this registration relates to a portable building for use as a garage as an entity, and is intended to depict the design of such a structure which has a conventional box-like middle portion with two specially shaped ends. As I have already indicated, the omission of the rear view is, in my judgment, of no significance, for all it would do would be to show a replica of that which is shown in the front view; nor, in my judgment, is it of any significance that in the central part of the structure certain windows are located. In my view that portion of the design is intended only to indicate an outline representation of a conventional structure, the windows of which may be varied at will.
>
> That the plaintiffs so intended their statement of novelty, referring as it does to having the ends coloured blue, in the plural, to relate to a structure in which both the front and rear were substantially identical is, as I think, clearly confirmed by the original statement which they submitted to the Registrar of Designs when they said 'the parts outlined in red'. Not that that original statement has any significance so far as the protection afforded by the design is concerned, but what it does do is that it confirms that the Registrar has properly acceded to their

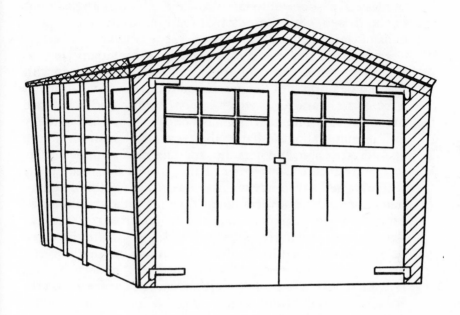

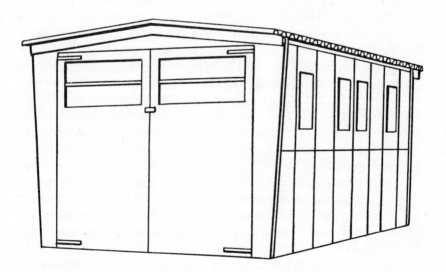

Fig. 3.11 Portable garage designs: (top) design as registered; (bottom) design held not to infringe

request, so expressed, so far as concerns securing registration of the design, with these design features applicable to both ends of the structure. . . .

The type of article sold by the defendant company [see the lower illustration redrawn in Fig. 3.11] . . . shows a body with the middle portion of a conventional form, to which is applied a front, the character of which I must now proceed to indicate in some detail. The structure has a pitched roof which is to my eye, perhaps, about 5° flatter than that which is shown in the registered design, and it has this special shaping applied solely to the front, the back being of the normal flat rectangular section. The splayed side members, as in the registered design, mark the ends of a rectangular opening which is closed by doors, but by reason of the lower pitch of the roof the height of the triangular pediment so formed is lower than in the registered design. There are in addition two quite minor differentiations which arise from the differing means of securing the termination of the roof projection, but I take the view that those are of only trifling significance.

Treated solely as fronts to garages, I myself entertain no doubt that these two differ in no substantial particular. That they are different is plain; but when one comes to consider the quantum of difference, especially having regard to the very distinctive outline which this type of construction permits, in my judgment they are substantially identical.

But the real distinction between the designs as applied to garages or portable buildings for use as garages arises, as I see it, from the presence of the design feature at both ends in the construction to which the registered design relates and only at the entrance end in the defendants' Senator construction. It is no doubt true that in actual use the entrance face of structures such as this will be more frequently observed, not only by the user but possibly also by passers-by and persons in the neighbourhood; but that, in my judgment, can be no proper reason for omitting the special shaping of the rear end when forming the mind's eye picture of the registered design, against which the question of infringement must necessarily be posed. To take a parallel, a substantial identity between the breeches or trousers and boots worn by two men would not obscure the marked differentiation that would be observable in their appearance, were one of them to have only one leg and the other two legs.

It has been held that there cannot be two registrations in respect of the same article differing only in statements claiming novelty for the shape of different parts because this would amount to seeking protection in respect of a part of an article.

By reason of what has been said in section 2.8 about no feature of a design being ignored completely, the effect of emphasizing or disclaiming portions of a design is not always predictable. A court is bound to, and does, take notice of the novelty claim but may not regard it as decisive, tending nevertheless to give some consideration to the claimed parts in relation to the design as a whole. One therefore wonders if a disclaimer entered during examination by direction of the Registrar is as restrictive as the Registrar would wish.

3.22 Illustrations

The illustrations of a design to be protected are the most important parts of a design application because it is principally these, in relation to the prior art, that define the scope of protection afforded by the registration and hence they also permit one to determine whether or not a competitor's design constitutes an infringement. They are discussed below under the separate headings of 'Representations' and 'Specimens' by which terms they are officially known. The present section concerns a few matters that affect both representations and specimens.

The Registrar may require the statement of novelty to be endorsed on the representations or specimens during the examination stage, but he seldom does so. If he were to exercise this prerogative more frequently, the courts might place greater emphasis on the novelty claim.

The minimum number of illustrations required is ascertainable from the last two columns of Fig. 3.9. If representations are filed, a specimen can be called for as well. Additional copies of the representations may also be required; they often are, for cross-reference purposes in the examiners' search files. In the case of a set of articles the illustrations must show the design applied to each article in the set.

It is repeated that words, letters and numerals not of the essence of the design should be omitted from the illustrations or neatly struck through. The same applies to electric leads for electrical equipment unless the leads somehow contribute to the eye-appeal.

If the design consists of a repeating surface pattern, the representations or specimens must show the complete pattern and some of the length and width of the repeat.

3.23 Specimens

There are few instances where it will be appropriate to file specimens. Except in cases of doubt, when the examiner requires to see a specimen (which can be returned) to understand the design or the article to which it is to be applied and to enable him to make suggestions as to how the applicant might clarify the illustrations or the specification of the article, specimens must be conveniently mountable in a flat condition by adhesive on paper or by stitching on linen-backed paper and they must be storable in a folder without damage to other documents. In practice, therefore, specimens are virtually confined to textile articles, wallpaper and lace. Specimens should never be smaller in size than 7 inch × 5 inch. If they are larger than 13 inch × 8 inch, they must be foldable to that size without damage. A specimen should not be regarded as a part taken as an example of the whole article. It should be a sample of the entire article (except in the case of textile piece goods).

3.24 Representations (contents)

One would think that it is common sense that the representations should fully and clearly illustrate the article to which the design is applied. The author recommends that they should do so, but a decided case where incomplete representations were accepted is described at the end of this section. For simple articles, a front perspective view from above and one side and a rear perspective view from below and the other side might be sufficient. For others (see Fig. 3.2), certain details of the design may not be evident without also filing a plan, underplan or elevation, or all three. Even an outline section or proper cross-sectional view might be necessary to reveal externally visible features of shape more clearly but in that case the cross-section should be blacked in on the plane of cut to obscure internal features that cannot normally be seen in the finished article.

The examiners at the Designs Registry do not consistently call for the same kind of views. It is sometimes so difficult to predict the official requirements that it is cheaper to file informal drawings such as blueprints with the application and then await a communication from the examiner before instructing the draughtsman to prepare proper design drawings or photographs. Alternatively, if there is sufficient time, the draughtsman (or photographer) could first be sent to the Designs Registry to discuss the required views with the examiner. In most cases, the examiners are quite reasonable in their demands, provided that the article is depicted fully and all the details of the design are reproduced, if necessary in enlarged views. There are firms who specialize in the preparation of patent and design drawings and photographs. By reason of their vast experience, they can often produce acceptable formal drawings even if they have only a thumbnail sketch to work from. What is more, they are thoroughly familiar with the official requirements in the UK and abroad and are moderate in their charges. Referring to the author's sketches of Fig. 3.1, his agents' draughtsman was requested to prepare formal design drawings for the UK from these sketches and within a day or so he was presented with the drawings of Fig. 3.2, which proved to be acceptable to the Designs Registry.

Attention is drawn to section 3.21 dealing with instances where the statement of novelty refers to marked portions of the representations. The marked representations are attached to the statement of novelty and are additional to the number of unmarked copies listed in Fig. 3.9. Section 3.21 also refers to the need for disclosing all the design features in the representations as originally filed (even if they are only informal representations) so as to avoid disclaimers. It is not possible to make substantial alterations to the illustrations after filing, except to correct an obvious mistake or to meet an official objection.

Should production difficulties or other circumstances demand a change to the design as first contemplated and as illustrated in the initial application papers and should it be desired to protect the new version specifically, there is simply no alternative to filing a fresh design application (if necessary under the provisions described in section 2.34, if the first design is also to proceed to registration). It is therefore advisable to delay filing of a design application (provided that this can be done without the danger of publication of the design in the meantime) until a production sample is available from which to prepare the representations, so that the design as registered will be the same as that of the article to be marketed by the applicant. Of course, there is nothing to compel a registered proprietor to use exactly the same design as is registered but it will be obvious that marked differences from the registered design will make it doubtful that the design as actually applied to the product is effectively protected by the design registration.

If the novelty of a design resides primarily or exclusively in the normally visible internal features of an article (as previously explained, normally invisible internal features are excluded from protection anyway), then external views of the article must nevertheless be included in the representations. This applies particularly to articles such as aeroplanes and caravans, where there must be a complete illustration of the exterior, while the interior would be shown by means of a side elevation with the doors open and/or a sectional plan view and/or a sectional side elevation. Views of the interior alone are not acceptable since the application would then be seeking protection for only a part of an article. The statement of novelty can draw specific attention to certain visible internal features but a court will also wish to pay attention to the external appearance when considering infringement.

Careful thought should be given to the question of including interior views in the representations. If the novelty resides mainly in the interior, there can be no doubt that interior pictures should be included, but not so when the exterior appearance is novel and the interior is of secondary importance. In an action concerning the cabinet for a record player, comprising a box with a lid in combination with a cupboard and doors, the trial judge had no doubt that the design protection extended to the interior of the cabinet because the photos showed the cabinet in the open and closed conditions. Although he considered that the exterior of a competitor's product was not materially different, the interior was so different that infringement had been successfully avoided.

Where the design is for the inside of a container that is sold with contents and has specially shaped receptacles in which the user will always loosely replace objects in a particular arrangement (e.g., a canteen for cutlery, a picnic basket or a tool box), the container must be illustrated without the contents because each application has to be in respect of a single article (or set).

Flexible or otherwise movable articles should be shown in the same position in all the views but one alternative position may be illustrated in an additional view. Articles of clothing are an exception to this rule of practice because they must always be shown laid out flat.

At the beginning of this section it was recommended that the representations should illustrate the entire article. This is the view that has been adopted by the Designs Registry and by the courts in the past. For example, the Court of Appeal once commented that if the result of the registered design is to leave it ambiguous whether a particular matter is included, you ought to turn the scales against the registered proprietor whose duty it is to make it perfectly clear what design it is in which he seeks a monopoly. In another case, the applicants for a design to be applied to a tramcar declined to file satisfactory representations. The views as filed consisted of a diagrammatic side elevation of the complete article and a diagrammatic end view of an incomplete article. The Registrar called for additional views illustrating the other side and other end, or a footnote to the effect that the other side and end corresponded to the filed views. His decision was supported on appeal.

More recently, however, the Registered Designs Appeal Tribunal has taken a more lenient view. Since the judgment raises important issues, extracts are given hereunder. The reader is invited to see whether he can find any flaws in the reasoning.

The appeal in this case raises an interesting and perhaps not wholly unimportant question. It is an appeal on application No. 945,141 under which number a design was applied for in respect of a wheel for a motor vehicle. It was supported by a representation in the form of a picture of what most of us would be able to recognize as a wheel for a motor vehicle as one normally sees such a wheel when removed from the car, that is to say, there is a tyre which is mounted upon some sort of rim which cannot be seen because it is obscured by the tyre, and then in the centre there is a support member for the rim which has decorative features . . . in a form which I understand is commonly known as 'a spider' where support members for the rim of varying shape radiate from a more or less solid member.

The illustration which has been supplied consists only of a view of the wheel as a whole plus the tyre as it would be seen by anybody looking at it from the side where it would be observed when mounted on the car. The Registrar thought in this case that further pictures or illustrations of the design in question should be supplied and called for such pictures or illustrations under the provisions of the Designs Rules.

The difficulty that the applicants are faced with is a practical difficulty because what the Registrar wanted was a view which would show the wheel without the tyre, and a view which would show perhaps the side of the wheel and the back of the wheel. At the time when the design was made it was no more than an artist's conception intended to be applied to a wheel and the exact form of the wheel when seen from the side without the tyre, or when seen from the back, had not been determined. The applicants, of course, wanted to secure their protection at the earliest possible date. . . .

I accept that there is a discretion and in this case the matter being one of discretion I am very conscious of the fact that the discretion has been exercised by an officer extremely experienced in this field who, as can be seen by reference to the long decision which has been given in this case, has considered the matter from every aspect and with the very greatest care . . . . Having considered the whole of this case, and the authorities which have been relied upon by the Registrar, I have come to the conclusion that the Registrar has in fact proceeded upon a wrong principle in this case and that the appeal should be allowed.

. . . but if no protection is being sought for the design features of the article at the side or back it does not seem to me there is any reason why there should be any representation of those aspects of the article at all. In fact I think it is thoroughly undesirable that the Register should be cluttered up with representations of features of articles which have got no significance from the point of view of the protection which is sought and which ought to have no significance in relation to the questions of infringement. . . .

In design cases the really important and significant question to my mind is: Does this application adequately show the design features which the applicant desires to protect in such a way that when he has secured his monopoly there will be no difficulty in ascertaining, when you look at the representation, what the design features are?

In truth to my mind in this case it is abundantly clear in the way the application has been framed that the appearance of the wheel from the side or the back is utterly irrelevant from the point of view of the claim to a design which has been made and in those circumstances inclusion of pictures of the side and the back would be a positive disadvantage.

I think myself it would even be a disadvantage to remove the tyre in the representation because as the design is now shown it is quite possible to form a very clear picture indeed as to what the area of the monopoly is, and any further exposure of those parts of the wheel, as to the design of which from the point of view of protection the applicants are wholly indifferent, could only produce doubt. I think the application ought to be allowed to proceed with the single representation in the form shown, save only for this, that I think the statement of novelty could be improved so that instead of reading 'the novelty resides in the shape and configuration of the wheel as shown in the representations', it should read 'the novelty resides in the shape and configuration of those parts of the wheel shown in the representation excluding the tyre and the parts marked with a blue cross', and it will then be apparent on the statement of novelty that no question of design features arises in relation to the side or the back, and with such a statement of novelty I think that really satisfactory protection will be given to the applicants, and satisfactory information given to anyone who may have to decide what the area of monopoly is.

It is not for the author of this book to criticize a judgment handed down by a court; but the reader should understand that considerable doubts have been expressed in the profession about the usefulness of a registration which is directed to only an inseparable part of an article, or part of the shape of an article, and, what is more, the design of which cannot be positively identified until an extraneous object (the tyre) has been placed on it. How easy will it be to enforce the registration in an infringement action? If the back of a competitor's wheel is perfectly plain, there might be no difficulty but if there are any striking features of shape or configuration on the back or rim, the sympathy of the court is likely to be with the alleged infringer.

With, perhaps, these doubts in mind, the Registry continues to call for additional views where the article has not been fully illustrated, but it will not insist on them if the applicant is unable or unwilling to lodge them.

3.25 Representations (formalities)

The representations of a design may be ink drawings, xerographs, or photographs; in other words, they must be permanent so that copies can still be made from them after many years. They may be in colour.

Each view of the representations should be appropriately designated 'plan', 'side elevation', 'enlarged end elevation', 'section

A–A', and so on. If a cross-section is filed, one of the other views should be referenced to show where the section has been taken. There are few instances where any further descriptive wording will be permitted on the representations. One exception is when the statement of novelty is required to be endorsed on the representations. Second, in order to keep the number of views to a minimum, footnotes may be included, such as 'The article is circular in plan', 'The article is of indefinite length and constant cross-section throughout', 'The article is of indefinite length and the shape and configuration between X–X and Y–Y is repeated throughout', 'The back of the article is plain' or 'The view from the other end corresponds'.

If photographic prints are filed, they should be mounted on 13 inch × 8 inch or A4 paper sheets with gum or adhesive and labelled with the designations of the views they represent. Reflections, shadows and distortions should be avoided and the article must be photographed against a plain background without showing any other object. In the case of drawings, these should be pictorial views making discreet use of shading and thick and thin lines. Production plans or blueprints showing dimensions, construction lines, guidelines or broken lines are definitely unacceptable. Nor must chain-dotted ghost lines be included to indicate the article in relation to other articles when in use. The drawings must be on stout paper and in ink, but photographic or xerographic prints of the ink drawings are preferred. Representations on tracing cloth or tracing linen should be mounted on paper. For printing type matrices, Designs Registry practice is to require that, in addition to representations of the matrices as such, imprints be filed of the type cast from the matrices so as to facilitate comparison with other designs.

3.26   Colour and finish

If coloured representations are filed, and especially if the colour is specifically claimed in the statement of novelty, colour will be taken into consideration in determining novelty and infringement, but only as one of the elements of the design. Colour alone does not constitute a registrable design feature. In this connection, it will be remembered that a design is defined as one of four visible features and colour is not one of these. However, colour can be one of the aspects of pattern or ornament and it will be evident that a difference in colour may be quite an important factor in some isolated instances, say in a design of checks and stripes applied to textile articles. A pattern of a plurality of concentric circles for a sunshade where alternate rings are coloured yellow and pink will clearly give a markedly different overall impression from one that is uncoloured or has alternate rings in dark blue and white. Much the same remarks apply to surface finishes or textures; a stippled surface can under certain circumstances make an article look strikingly different from a glossy one. To quote a judge in a High Court action concerning textile designs, 'You may have a design which is unobtrusive in certain colours. There is no difficulty in certain cases in having designs with the same background but in which differences of colour might produce very different

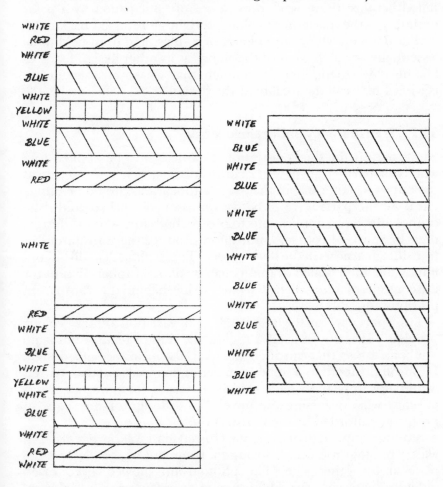

Fig. 3.12 Two textile designs of coloured stripes; registrations declared valid

appearances. Colour cannot be disregarded; it may or may not make a material difference'.

Referring to Fig. 3.12, both of the illustrated designs featuring in a court case consisted of plain stripes of varying thickness and were registered in respect of textile piece goods, handkerchiefs and shawls. One design consisted of only blue stripes separated by uncoloured strips. The second design was more complex. The validity of these designs was put in dispute in an infringement action. The allegedly infringing designs were identical with the two registered designs in all respects. The defendants pleaded generally that a pattern of plain stripes cannot be the subject matter of a valid registration for a new or original design but their pleadings failed because there was no evidence of anticipation by a prior design. On the question of colour, the judge referred back to an earlier decision where the colours of a shawl had been held to be 'essentially as much parts of the shawl' as its other design features and he added to this his own comment that 'what appeals to the eye is what I may call the totality of the design'.

3.27   Transparency and translucency

An applicant for the registration of a design to be applied to a wholly or partly transparent or translucent article must decide at the outset whether or not the overall appearance would be different if all the parts were to be shown as opaque. If so, and if he cannot afford two applications to protect both forms of the design, then he must, of course, faithfully reproduce the transparent or translucent aspects in the illustrations. This is difficult to do but not impossible for a skilled draughtsman or photographer. Except for the contents of a container, the parts visible behind the transparent portion must also be reproduced.

Transparency can be regarded as a variation of the 'colour problem'. It is not in itself a registrable design feature but is no doubt an aspect that can affect the overall appearance of a design. It is brought about by a suitable choice of materials but that in itself would not appear to be a sufficient reason for ignoring transparency when assessing the novelty of a design or the scope of protection afforded by the registration.

A design applied to ornamental frosted glass was once registered with a photograph taken through a fragment of the glass onto a plate at the other side. The photograph showed a 'confused indeterminate pattern'. The judge in an infringement trial commented that the photograph did not show what you will see when the glass is held up to the light and when you look through it. What you saw in the photograph was that which appeared on the plate behind it. This case demonstrates that it is important to illustrate the design in the form in which it appears to the viewer of the article.

Bubble packs, being transparent containers that so closely envelop the contents (and to some extent assume their shape) that they must be destroyed to release the contents, have already been referred to in section 3.18.

3.28 Secrecy order

For security reasons, an absolute or partial secrecy order may be applied by the Registrar to designs relevant for defence purposes. Contravention of the order can result in imprisonment, or a fine, or both. The author has often encountered secrecy orders on patents for inventions but never on designs. It is, however, just conceivable that someone might develop a weapon or a piece of equipment for a nuclear physics laboratory with not only functional but also eye-catching considerations in mind; in that case there could be a desire to keep the design secret, especially if the appearance of the article necessarily reveals to the viewer something about the construction or function that is of national importance.

4. Examination and registration

4.1 Office practice

After an application has been filed, accompanied by at least informal representations and the full amount of the government fee, a filing receipt is issued (see Fig. 3.6) giving the filing date and application number. This number stays the same throughout the life of the application and subsequent registration. The application will then be officially examined as quickly as the Designs Registry's workload permits.

The Registrar (or his examining staff) may refuse an application on one or more of the many grounds discussed in previous sections, in particular that the application is not for a design within the meaning of the Act or industrially applied to an article or set of articles covered by the Act, that the design is illegal or immoral, or that it is not novel or original. He may also raise formal objections which can and must be overcome by the applicant before registration can take place, for example in connection with the particulars given on the application form or the wording of the statement of novelty or the form and contents of the representations.

For the purpose of determining novelty, the Registrar may conduct a search and in fact he does so for most applications (check, stripe and lace designs excepted) but his resources are limited. Although he employs examiners to do the searching for him and to conduct correspondence with the applicant or the applicant's agent, his staff is not so large as to permit an exhaustive novelty search to be carried out. To do so would in any case require an impossibly extensive collection of British and foreign periodicals and trade literature, of which every illustration on each page would have to be carefully classified and cross-referenced. In practice, therefore, the official novelty search is restricted to prior UK design registrations and a few recent periodicals.

The Appeal Tribunal has recognized the Registrar's limited financial and other resources by agreeing that the Registrar may dispute novelty without citing a particular publication or purchasing a sample to prove that a design is common. The Tribunal remarked:

> Where, as so often is the case, the real measure of comparison is as between the design submitted for registration and a commonly accepted design in any particular art, the more common the knowledge as to the general features of design in the trade, the more difficult it may be to secure representations of such design in current literature. So far as I know, there are no public funds available which would justify the Patent Office in procuring physical embodiments of common designs for the purpose of demonstrating to a dissatisfied applicant particular features of common general knowledge, and it is, I suppose, not unreasonable to assume, so far as representations are concerned, that it is only if the Office is fortunate in tracing a representation put out by someone who thinks that it might serve his interest—a position which becomes less and less likely the more the design is common to the trade—that examination of catalogues, textbooks and the like will enable the Patent Office to produce a visual indication.

This ruling is difficult to reconcile with an earlier judgment by a higher court, namely the Chancery of the County Palatine of Lancaster, in a case where the defendants had copied a design of stripes for cotton piece goods. They pleaded in their defence: 'In the cotton trade and in particular in the export trade to West Africa, such arrangements have been commonplace for many years prior to the alleged registration by the plaintiffs.' The Vice Chancellor queried the absence of particular anticipations and said 'It seems to me that, when a statement is made in a pleading that it is a matter of common knowledge, then of course you do not give particulars; you can refer to books; but when you are dealing with a question of novelty and in fact that the design has been anticipated by some particular other design, you must give particulars.'

In the author's view, it is unsound that particulars of anticipation are not required during examination but must be given in a trial before the court. Nevertheless, the Registry still relies on the

Appeal Tribunal's remarks today when making unsupported general criticisms on novelty and originality during examination.

On occasions, an examiner might wish to cite an as yet unpublished pending prior application as a ground for objecting to a conflicting second application. This is not possible, so he will usually try to ensure that registration of the second application is delayed (by postponing examination) until the first application has matured into a registration and can be validly cited (see section 2.27 for the case where the second application happens to be registered first). It may also happen that a prior registered but as yet unpublished design (see section 5.13) stands in the way of an application. The applicant will then need to see whether the official objection is justified and he does so in the presence of the Registrar.

If an application is refused, the Registrar's decision at the hearing is subject to appeal.

4.2 Procedure

Objections are communicated by the examiner in writing about one to three months from the filing date (on occasions, even within two weeks, depending on the workload of particular examiners, although lately there have been delays of well over six months) and amendments or arguments to overcome the objections are then lodged, usually also in writing; however, a hearing may be appointed if no agreement is reached. To argue against a novelty objection, a hearing must be requested within one month of the letter of objection or a request should be filed for an extension of time. In cases where there is reasonable doubt as to whether or not a design or the application submitted for registration satisfies official requirements, the benefit of the doubt is given to the applicant (at his own risk, because a judge might conceivably rule against the registered proprietor if the validity of the design is later disputed in court). There is also a provision enabling the Registrar to correct errors in an application (including the representations) on a request filed voluntarily by the applicant or on the Registrar's own volition. Especially in connection with the representations, alterations can only be allowed to correct obvious mistakes recognizable from the papers as originally filed.

As the time when the Designs Registry can commence examination of an application and the promptness with which the applicant attends to the official objections depend on so many variables, not considering the pressure of business in the office of any design registration agent who may be consulted, it is impossible to forecast how long it might take before a particular application matures to a registration. Unobjectionable applications could have their registration certificates granted after only one to three months; applications on which the objections are overcome quickly may take an additional three weeks; but many applications take about four to five months (except in the recent past, when extraordinary delays have occurred at the Designs Registry). The registration certificate of Fig. 3.7 issued just under six weeks from the filing date but could have issued sooner; a delay was caused by the file being considered by a senior examiner who telephoned the applicant's design agent and expressed a doubt that any eye-appeal was intended for such a functional design. The examiner did not persist with the objection, so a hearing was not necessary.

4.3 Time limits

To save an application from abandonment, it should be completed within 12 months from the UK filing date, or within 15 months subject to a monthly fine payable with an application for extension of time. If the term expires on a Saturday, Sunday or holiday, it is automatically extended to the next following business day. The 15 months can be enlarged still further if the Registrar thinks fit but, unless the circumstances are most exceptional or a delay occurred at the Designs Registry, the Registrar will not exercise his discretion in favour of the applicant.

Irrespective of the overall time limit, an application is deemed to be abandoned if a hearing is not requested within one month of the date of an official novelty objection, or any extended period allowed by the Registrar.

4.4 Appeals

Appeals from the Registrar's decisions, except on the questions of whether a series of articles constitutes a set and whether a textile design consists mainly of checks or stripes, lie to the Appeal Tribunal, which is constituted by a High Court judge experienced in matters affecting the protection of industrial property. The Appeal Tribunal may examine witnesses on oath, award costs and exercise any power that could have been exercised by the Registrar in the proceedings below.

4.5 Registration certificate

There is no opposition period for enabling interested third parties to object to a design application. A certificate of registration (see the example in Fig. 3.7) is issued to the design proprietor as soon as he has complied with all the formalities and overcome any official objection. This certificate is a valuable document and should be kept in a safe place because it is *prima facie* proof of ownership of the design registration and the rights accruing from it. A duplicate can be issued only upon payment of a fee and filing of a statutory declaration or affidavit setting out the full circumstances concerning the loss or destruction of the original. The certificate differs in wording depending on whether the application was filed with or without a claim to priority under the provisions of the International Convention and whether the design is an associated design. It has attached to it one of the representations or specimens that was supplied by the applicant. Infringements of the design committed before issue of the registration certificate are not actionable. If a registration is surrendered (cancelled by the Registrar on request by the proprietor, as distinct from being allowed to lapse by failing to renew the registration for a further term), the certificate of registration must be returned to the Designs Registry.

4.6 Date of registration

A design is registered as of the UK filing date or some earlier or later date directed by the Registrar and it is this registration date from which the term of protection and renewal dates are calculated. The date of registration of a Convention application is the priority date, i.e., the first foreign filing date from which priority was claimed for the British application.

Apart from Convention applications, it is comparatively rare for the Registrar to direct that the date of registration should be earlier than the filing date, but it does happen. One instance is where an application is filed in respect of a set of articles and the Registrar rules that the articles do not qualify as a set. Since the applicant will have illustrated the designs of all the articles in the representations accompanying the application and the designs may already have been published by the time the objections to a 'set' are officially communicated, the Registrar may—but he is under no obligation to do so—permit the original application to be divided into an appropriate number of separate applications each of which will attract the normal filing fee and each of which will be accorded a filing date when this fee is paid. It may then be directed by the Registrar that the dates of registration of the divisional applications be antedated to the filing date, or Convention priority date, of the 'set' application.

Similar considerations might apply where a proprietor inadvertently files an application in respect of more than one article, i.e., where he thought that only one article was involved. This is a mistake that is not so unusual as one might at first think, especially in view of the anomalies indicated in section 3.18. A canteen for cutlery was an example mentioned in that section. Any other kind of container with readily accessible contents falls into the same category; the contents are articles different and separate from the container and must be protected in separate applications, but the applicant may not have known this at the time of filing. A mistake might also occur when the design is for, say, a multi-purpose tool comprising a handle and several alternative attachments; while the tool with a single attachment in position would be permitted in one application, the other attachments are regarded as separate articles. In all cases where a design application is mistakenly filed in respect of more than one article, it will need to be divided and the Registrar may, in his discretion, direct a registration date earlier than the actual filing date for each divisional application.

An example of a registration date later than the actual filing date does not readily come to mind; in fact it is doubtful that a design application has ever been post-dated. Post-dating is not likely to be an alternative to a disclaimer of design features that were not disclosed in the original application papers; the only alternative to a disclaimer is the filing of a new application which attracts another application fee. Applications which are incomplete to begin with are not accorded a filing date until they are complete so, again, there is no question of post-dating.

5. *After registration*

5.1 Term of registration

The maximum period for which a design registration can remain in force in the UK is 15 years from the date of registration and it is repeated that the date of registration is not to be confused with the date on which the registration certificate issued. For an associated design, the term is limited to the unexpired term of the parent registration. Initially, the term of protection for an ordinary registration is five years without paying anything additional to the application fee, but renewal of the term is possible for two further periods of five years each as described later. In the case of a design that corresponds to an artistic work and was registered only by reason of the exempting provisions explained previously, the term of the registration cannot exceed the period of artistic copyright, i.e., the registration will expire either 15 years from the registration date or with expiry of the artistic copyright, whichever is the earlier.

Since the design registration has a direct bearing on production and a company may possess several registrations relating to various products, some form of abridged documentation may be desirable for quick reference to avoid the need for searching through an entire file of correspondence every time a question arises. If a good filing system is already in existence, a separate sheet or card for the important particulars need not be kept separate; the particulars can be entered in the form of a checklist on the cover of the file in question. Otherwise, it is recommended that a separate subject index be started for internal administration purposes. Desirably, a schedule should list the name by which the product is known, the application or priority date of the design application, its number, the date of issue of the registration certificate and brief details about copyright (section 7.18 includes a summary of the vital statistics that should be kept); as and when the term of the registration is renewed, this information should also be included in the checklist.

5.2 Renewal

The initial term of the registration can be extended by paying a renewal fee and a final five year extension is again subject to the payment of a renewal fee (see section 5.32 for a discussion on costs). The renewal fee can be paid late if a fine is also paid—but in no circumstances later than six months after expiry of the relevant five year period. For an associated design, renewal must be sought before expiration of the current term of the parent registration or within the six month period of grace. If the application for the associated design is still unregistered at the time the parent registration is due for renewal, the parent registration should be renewed and a request for renewing the pending application must also be lodged.

It will be appreciated that there is a six month period during which the public may be in doubt as to whether or not a proprietor intends to renew the term of his registration by late payment of the fee. There is no provision for protecting third parties who avail themselves of the design in the mistaken belief that the design registration has ceased (but see the remarks on innocent infringers in section 5.28). Once the six month late payment period has expired, there is no way whatsoever of restoring the lapsed registration. This is in sharp contrast with patent law. The Registrar's discretionary powers to enlarge times do not extend to such statutory periods.

Renewal fees may be budgeted well in advance of the due date, in fact immediately after issue of the registration certificate if so desired, but there is little to recommend this practice because it is impossible to forecast whether a design will prove to be sufficiently successful in commerce to merit the expense of protection for a second or third five year term. At one time, a doubtful advantage of actually paying renewal fees in advance was that one might thereby save a few pounds if the renewal fees were increased in the intervening period but, more recently, the registered proprietor has been asked to make up the difference. It is important for the design owner to diarize the renewal dates; but if he employs an agent, he will not generally have to bother about this because a free reminder service is provided by most agents.

The vast majority of design registrations falls by the wayside after the initial five year term, not because of any misgivings on the part of the proprietors about the amount of the renewal costs but because many products are out of date after five years or so. Nevertheless, very approximately one registration in three is renewed once, and of these about one in three is kept alive for the maximum term. Renewal fees are good value for money and if, at the time a renewal fee falls due for payment, the proprietor finds that the line is still selling well, he will not mind paying a little extra to preserve a monopoly for his products.

5.3 The register of designs

The register of designs is a multi-volume book kept at the Designs Registry for recording the name and address of the proprietor, notices of any assignments and licences, the address for service, the date of application, the date as of which the design is registered, the date on which the certificate of registration issued, the specification of the article for which the design is registered and notices of renewals. The register can be inspected on payment of a small fee and certified copies are obtainable. The register does not give an illustration of the design; nor does it contain the statement of novelty. Errors in the particulars entered in the register may be corrected. Other alterations can also be effected if any of the registered particulars happen to undergo a change, but proof may be required.

5.4 Right given by registration

The right given by a design registration is a monopoly. The registered proprietor is said to have the exclusive right in the United Kingdom of Great Britain, Northern Ireland and the Isle of Man to make or import for sale or for use for the purposes of any trade or business, or to sell, hire, or offer for sale or hire, any article in respect of which the design is registered and to which the registered design or a substantially similar design has been applied, and to make anything for enabling any such article to be made. This is more or less what is stated in the Designs Act and this seems to be the major reason why the uninitiated often labour under a misapprehension. Time and again a manufacturer will instruct his agent that no effort should be spared in obtaining a registration for his design despite the existence of a competitor's similar design because he mistakenly believes that, if he is successful in obtaining a registration of his own, he will enjoy exclusive rights for the design. The truth is that no exclusive rights are granted by the registration at all. If the design is valid and enforcible (but there is no guarantee that this will be so, since the official novelty search is a very limited one) then the only right that the proprietor enjoys is to stop others from making, importing, selling and so on, i.e., to stop others from infringing his registration, but by no means can he be certain that by marketing articles bearing his registered design he will not be infringing someone else's registration. An applicant for registration should therefore not be under the illusion (a) that the grant of the registration is a guarantee of validity and (b) that the registration enables him to exploit the design without regard to his competitors' rights.

Regardless of validity or the possibility of infringement, the proprietor of a design has the right—subject to the rights vested in any other person whose interest is entered in the register in respect of that design—to deal with the design by assignment or licence. The responsibility is usually that of the purchaser or licensee to ensure by appropriate investigations and searches that what he is buying is worthwhile. After the assignment or licence has been signed, the purchaser will find it difficult to dispute the validity of the design, unless the vendor or licensor had foolishly guaranteed that the registration is valid and would not infringe an earlier registration.

A design registration does not affect the right of the Crown to sell or use articles forfeited under the customs or excise laws (for Crown rights also see the section on compulsory licences).

5.5 Transfer of design rights

Designs can be sold or licensed. The consideration is usually a once-and-for-all payment or a royalty, or both, but other kinds of remuneration are also possible. An outright sale (assignment) involves transfer to the purchaser of some or all of the rights in the registration possessed by the proprietor, the purchaser thereby becoming the new proprietor or a part-proprietor. An assignment could provide for reversion of the rights to the original proprietor after a prescribed time or if certain conditions are not fulfilled. A licence amounts to permission from the proprietor to exercise any or all of the rights in the registration, the ownership of the registration remaining unchanged even if the licence is an exclusive one, i.e., exclusive of the proprietor himself.

In theory, an assignment or licence is not possible until after the registration certificate has issued because until then no rights are in existence that could be assigned or licensed, except the previously discussed right to file the design application in the first place or the right to claim priority for a design application to be filed under the provisions of the International Convention. However, an agreement can be concluded at any time to assign or to license the design after registration has taken place and royalties may also be made payable before registration. The assignment is eventually effected by means of a Deed, which means a document executed under seal, and it may have to be stamped by the Inland Revenue authorities. The sale or licensing of industrial property rights attracts Value Added Tax which is recoverable by the assignee or licensee only if he is a registered trader.

The Designs Registry, unlike the Patent Office, has no power to allow a pending design application to proceed in a new name by reason of any transfer of ownership that has taken place after the application date, except in the case where an applicant dies. When the registration certificate has issued, anyone who acquires a registered design or a share in or licence under the registration must apply to have his interest recorded in the register. The Act makes this obligatory, although it is not clear what the penalty might be for failure to comply. As an alternative, the assignor or licensor may apply to have the change recorded. In either case, proof of title must be given. Practical disadvantages of failing to record a change of ownership, or failing to record it promptly, include: (a) the new owner will not be able to enforce his rights; (b) only the old owner or his agent will be officially reminded of renewal fees or receive other correspondence; (c) where a request for recording an interest in a design is filed more than six months from the date of acquisition, the government fee for recordal is higher, and still higher after twelve months; (d) if the Designs Registry is not happy with the wording of the assignment for recording purposes, objections are normally sorted out straight away; if the Registry does not see the assignment until much later, the signatories may no longer be available to clarify or rectify ambiguities or errors; (e) no licence from the assignee to a third party can be recorded until after the assignee's own rights in the design have been recorded.

In the case of acquisitions by inheritance, Letters Probate or Letters of Administration must be obtained and it will be the executor or administrator who assigns the registration to the rightful heir.

Under the Patents Act, certain contracts can be terminated if three months' notice is given after the patent has ceased to be in force, no matter what the contract might say to the contrary. There is no similar provision under design law, so design agreements should be particularly carefully worded in this respect, although it could be argued that a licence granted solely under a design registration will be in restraint of trade if it continues beyond the life of the registration, i.e., if it requires the licensee to make royalty payments after other manufacturers are already free to use the design because the registration has expired.

As to the form that a licence or assignment should take, this will depend on the particular commercial considerations. No one other than a solicitor or barrister with specialized knowledge of industrial property matters should be relied on to draft an appropriate document or to adapt a previous draft to meet different circumstances, but a design agent can be helpful in negotiating the terms by conducting, or being present at, the discussions.

5.6 Restrictive practices

Licences and assignments should preferably avoid restrictive clauses which do not concern articles to which the design is applied. An agreement between two or more persons carrying on business in the UK is subject to registration under the Restrictive Trade Practices Act 1976 if, under the agreement, any express or implied restriction (or obligation, privilege or benefit) is accepted by two or more parties in respect of, *inter alia*, the prices of goods and the process of manufacture to be applied to goods. A licence or assignment granted by the proprietor of a design, or any agreement for such a licence or assignment, is exempt from registration under the Restrictive Trade Practices Act only if it contains no such restriction or the restriction is confined to articles in respect of which the design is being or has been registered. By reason of the Fair Trading Act 1973, design pooling agreements are also required to be registered.

It is important to remember that, if agreements are concluded with foreign nationals, the laws of the other countries will also have to be taken into consideration. The law against unfair competition is one which merits particular attention abroad. Caution should also be exercised regarding possible anti-trust laws and foreign counterparts of the UK Restrictive Trade Practices Act, especially in the Common Market, where provision is made for lodging agreements with the EEC Commission and doing so could prevent dire consequences if an objectionable clause is found to exist. The danger of including licensing conditions which are tantamount to restraint of trade is far smaller in the UK than, say, in the US where the anti-trust law severely limits the area of agreement. The mere mention of collaboration between two companies gives rise to suspicion in America. A design registration in the US is termed a Design Patent and it is subject to the same anti-trust law as is a patent for invention. The underlying basis of the anti-trust law is to prohibit the monopoly obtained by the patent from being extended to unpatentable ideas and know-how and generally to prevent situations from arising that inhibit competition. In order to steer clear of conflict with the US anti-trust law, British design proprietors should in their negotiations with US firms be careful to avoid cross-licences and refrain from inserting clauses in the licence that regulate the procurement of materials, or deal with cooperation in allied fields, the exclusion of competition, the sale of know-how, price fixing, restriction on resale, and so on. Trade mark licences should always be divorced from agreements on US design patents. In the EEC, too, certain contractual obligations may be regarded as impermissible restrictive trade practices which used to be perfectly legal in the UK—for example, an undertaking by the licensee not to dispute the validity of the licensed design registration. In general, the limitations are most severe in the US and least severe in the UK. In many South American countries it is not even possible to conclude a licence without government sanction by way of a compulsory recording procedure that aims to supervise foreign control or dominance and to preserve the extravagant use of foreign currency.

5.7 Assignments

When a solicitor is eventually consulted in connection with engrossing an assignment, the client should be clear as to the following points in addition to the price that has been agreed.

(a) Which rights in the registration are being assigned?
(b) Is the assignee also to receive the right to file corresponding foreign design applications, with or without the right to claim

priority from the British application under the provisions of the International Convention?

(c) Is the assignee entitled to sue for any past infringements?
(d) Is the artistic copyright in the original plans and/or in the article to which the design is applied also being assigned?
(e) Who is to pay for recording the assignment at the Designs Registry?

The deed of assignment for recording in the UK should mention a tolerably accurate monetary consideration which is commensurate with the true commercial value of the design. This is in contrast with many other countries, where a nominal consideration may be referred to, for example '$1 and other good and valuable consideration'. Exceptions arise where the design is being assigned to a wholly owned subsidiary company, or vice versa, or where the assignor was holding the design in trust for the assignee or where the assignment can be regarded as a genuine gift. Under those circumstances, the consideration is not monetary and the deed may also be exempt from stamp duty. Whenever the assignment does not form part of a transaction of which the value exceeds £15 000 or £20 000 or £25 000 or £30 000, as the case may be, this fact should be mentioned in the deed to save on stamp duty.

5.8 Licences

Licences tend to be much more complicated arrangements than assignments because many more considerations are involved. A solicitor will need to know his client's wishes in respect of the following details before he can draft a suitable document (NB: it is not pretended that this list is exhaustive).

(a) Which activities are to be licensed and which excluded?
(b) Is there to be any restriction on
    (i) quality?
    (ii) how the design is applied?
    (iii) territory of manufacture?
    (iv) sales territory?
    (v) departure from the design as registered?
(c) Is the licence to be
    (i) exclusive (which means exclusive of everyone—even the proprietor himself)?
    (ii) non-exclusive (which leaves scope for further licences)?
    (iii) sole (i.e., exclusive except of the registered proprietor)?

(d) Is it permissible to
   (i) sub-licence?
   (ii) assign the licence?
(e) Is the remuneration to include a lump sum down-payment?
(f) What is the percentage royalty to be and how is it to be calculated (e.g., on net ex-works price before charging Value Added Tax, insurance, packing, trade discounts and commissions etc.)?
(g) Is there to be a 'best endeavours' clause (requiring the licensee to do his utmost to commercialize the design), or a minimum total royalty per annum or some time limit by which production is to commence?
(h) Is royalty payable on all articles made, all articles delivered to customers or only those articles actually sold and/or paid for?
(i) At what time intervals is royalty payable, in which currency and to what bank?
(j) What marking in addition to the registered design number is required (e.g., 'Made under licence from. . . .')?
(k) What is the duration of the licence and how may it be terminated prematurely?
(l) Are infringements to be actionable by the licensee (jointly with the licensor) and, if so, at whose expense?
(m) How are disputes in connection with the licence agreement to be settled and under the law of which country?
(n) What accounts are to be kept and by whom can they be inspected?
(o) Who selects and pays for corresponding foreign design registrations?
(p) Has the licensee first refusal on future designs developed by the licensor for the same or different articles?
(q) Is there to be any technical assistance, and, if so, in what form?
(r) Who is to be responsible for stamping the licence and recording it at the Designs Registry?

A licence that is at the outset negotiated willingly by both parties is more likely to be successful than not. Both a licensor and a licensee stand to profit from continuing to cooperate with one another in the spirit of the licence agreement and even beyond it—the licensee by increasing his sales and the licensor by collecting correspondingly more money in royalties. If the licensor comes to learn of better production techniques or improvements in the design, he would therefore be foolish to withhold the information from the other contracting party. He might first try to extract a higher royalty from the licensee, or conclude a separate agreement that is the subject of separate royalties. He might even find a different interested manufacturer to do business with if he can terminate the first agreement, although he will tend to adopt the attitude of 'better the devil you know, than the one you do not'. Eventually, however, he can be expected to exploit his improvement to the best advantage by parting with it to some licensee, and that licensee will reciprocate with goodwill towards the licensor. Both parties will use their best endeavours to make the agreement work well and to be financially successful in the business venture.

Not so with an agreement that is concluded reluctantly by one of the parties. A licensor who may be compelled to give a licence, for example a compulsory licence as referred to in section 5.17, or a royalty-free licence granted as a 'bribe' in return for not nullifying the design registration, cannot be expected to give of his best—to keep the licensor supplied with up-to-date information on production techniques or anything else. On the contrary, the licensor will do his utmost to get out of the agreement or to find loopholes, whereby the whole association will become unpalatable to the licensee. The same applies to a reluctant licensee who is dependent on the registered proprietor for a licence because he is obliged to make the protected design for commercial reasons; he will spend increasingly more time in endeavouring to break the licence. Nevertheless, occasions arise where licences must be concluded reluctantly and it is then even more important to exercise extreme care and caution in wording the agreement because the reluctant signatory is bound to prove obstructive.

Practically all the points in a licence agreement are variable, that is to say, they can be tailored to meet particular requirements and wishes. If there is a will to agree, a way can be found. This is where skilful bargaining and a knowledge of the possibilities is essential. Thus, a design proprietor may have high hopes of being able to exploit his design widely through several manufacturers spread throughout the country, thereby being assured of saturating the market and collecting more in royalties, on the understanding that competition between the several manufacturers is healthy and will boost sales. The first prospective licensor to be approached, however, endeavours to ensure that the licence is exclusive to him; he is not prepared to invest in the machinery or incur the tooling costs if his territory is limited or if he has to compete with other manufacturers in the same territory. On first appearances, the negotiators may at this stage be at loggerheads but compromises may by all means be possible to prevent the discussions from foundering. Provided that one of the parties (or one of the advisers sitting in) is sufficiently astute or experienced, it will be realized that for an initial term the licence can be exclusive and, after a specified time, the licence changes to a non-exclusive one if the licensee fails to live up to expectations.

In the same way, many of the other terms of a licence are flexible. There need not be a royalty, or there can be only a nominal royalty to start with but a correspondingly higher royalty after a specified term. The territory may be restricted at first and limitless after the licensee has shown what he can do. The duration of the agreement need not be for a set number of years but can be indefinite (usually for the life of the design registration) or until such time as one party gives a certain period of written notice to the other. All sorts of variations are possible on major issues. Even the minor ones are open to variation by negotiation. For example, if the licensee does not wish to have his books inspected by the licensor, a mutually acceptable independent third party can be appointed to do so.

5.9   Cancellation of registration by Registrar

Subject to any appeal, the Registrar is empowered to cancel a registration on request by an 'interested' person. The grounds of cancellation are that the design was not new or original at the date of registration, that the design corresponds to an artistic work for which copyright has already expired, or any other ground on which the registration could have been refused by the Registrar in the first place. In the cancellation proceedings, the Registrar may award costs and he can also require security for costs to be given by the person who initiates the proceedings if that person neither lives nor works in the UK. Evidence before the Registrar is given by affidavit or statutory declaration and/or orally. Witnesses may be cross-examined. The required interest in initiating cancellation proceedings must be real. It is not sufficient for the applicant for cancellation to plead that he wishes to see justice done. Nor can the applicant be a nominee acting for a party that wishes to remain anonymous. The applicant could be someone who claims to be the rightful owner of the design or who is in business in the same kind of articles as are the subject of the registration. A business interest will nearly always be sufficient, provided this exists in the UK. Guidance in this respect may be obtained from patent law where an opponent to the grant of Letters Patent must likewise show a *bona fide* interest.

The procedure in cancellation proceedings is also much the same as for patent oppositions. The applicant for cancellation lodges a statement of the facts on which he relies. If the proprietor wishes to defend his registration, he lodges his arguments in a counterstatement. It is then the applicant's turn to file evidence in support of his case, followed by counter-evidence from the proprietor, whereupon the applicant has another chance to lodge evidence which is strictly in reply to the counter-evidence. A hearing is then appointed, which may be in public and at which the parties may be represented by Counsel.

Cancellation proceedings are not common occurrences. Where a competitor's invalid registration proves to be a real obstacle—for example, if he intimidates existing or potential customers and seriously jeopardizes one's own business—cancellation may be the only solution; but usually a competent design agent will be able to suggest less costly alternative courses of action. One currently popular approach of questionable propriety for arriving at an amicable settlement is to seek a royalty-free licence under the allegedly invalid design registration in return for not initiating cancellation proceedings. In this way the parties effectively agree to share the market between them and use the supposedly invalid registration to keep others out. Another possibility is to ignore the objectionable design registration until such time as its proprietor takes the initiative; one can then try to persuade him that his registration is unenforcible. A great deal depends on the particular circumstances of each case and the best solution will not become apparent until it has been established precisely what evidence of invalidity is available.

5.10 Rectification of register by court

As a far more costly alternative to cancellation proceedings before the Registrar, an 'aggrieved' person may petition the court to rectify the register by making, varying or deleting an entry in it. In this case the Registrar is informed and he may also be heard. The grounds for seeking a rectification order will usually be the same as those that can be pleaded before the Registrar but the end effect may be different. Whereas in cancellation proceedings the Registrar can only decide to cancel the registration or to let it stand, the court may also order the insertion or variation of entries in the register. For example, if someone thinks that the design was obtained from him against his rights and he should have been the proprietor, the court could order that the aggrieved person's name be substituted for that of the registered proprietor. It is also conceivable that the court may order correction of the specification of the article given in the register if the registered designation for some reason aggrieves the applicant, e.g., if a trade mark is inadvertently used to describe the article.

More often than not, an application for rectification by the court will be lodged by a defendant as a counter claim in infringement proceedings whereas an application for cancellation to the Registrar is the preferred form of action in cases where infringement proceedings are not pending. An 'aggrieved' person would seem to mean more than the 'interested' person in cancellation proceedings in so far that he should, to have a *bona fide* interest, be adversely affected by the matter that is sought to be rectified.

There is one aspect that can be raised for consideration in both cancellation and rectification proceedings but not during examination of an application, and that is commercial success. Of course, commercial success is no proof that a design is new or original and therefore validly registered but, as readers familiar with litigation in patent matters will know, it can be another argument in support of validity. In an action in 1893, popularity and large sales immediately after marketing the articles were in fact taken into account when the novelty of the design for a toilet basin was disputed.

5.11   Scare value of a registration

The application form that is required to be filed at the Designs Registry contains a claim to the proprietorship of the design in question. Not infrequently, the applicant puts tongue in cheek and claims to own the design when in reality he does not. He may have obtained the design by way of a sample article from a foreign owner on the pretext of being interested in importing the foreign-made articles to the UK, whereas his intention was really to set up manufacture on his own. Before commencing production, he then files a British design application claiming to be the proprietor of the design. As another example, it frequently happens that a British manufacturer will find an interesting product on sale in a foreign city. He buys one, brings it back and, again, files a UK design application in his own name. Under these and similar circumstances, a registration will most probably be granted to the UK applicant because the British examiner is unlikely to suspect that the applicant is not the lawful proprietor of the design. However, the resultant design registration is invalid. The problem is, who is to know? Of course, the foreign design owner would know but, if and when he becomes aware of the UK design registration, he may be loth to spend a lot of money on having the invalid registration struck off. The foreign owner can be expected to ignore the registration and sell in competition with the British manufacturer but in the meantime the invalid design registration remains on the UK register and has the effect of scaring off third parties who might have been interested in making the same articles but who have no means of knowing the true position.

It is impossible to estimate how many designs are filed and registered for their scare value. The author believes that very few knowingly pass through the hands of agents because it is an agent's duty not to aid and abet in making a false claim in the application form; but there may be a significant number of self-filed invalid registrations and there seems to be no effective way of stopping such malpractice.

A false declaration is not involved in filing a design application which is no longer new because of, say, prior sale or disclosure by the proprietor of articles bearing the design. Although the resulting registration is nevertheless invalid, it is, again, frequently used for its scare value.

5.12 Official publication

Abandoned or refused design applications remain unpublished for all time as far as the Designs Registry is concerned but naturally there is nothing to stop the proprietor from making details of the design known (and he very often does so by marketing articles bearing the design). By way of exception, a refused design of a human figure was published in the report of the previously mentioned Departmental Committee on Industrial Designs. It is reproduced from the report at the left-hand side in Fig. 5.1 and, when the Committee compared it with the accepted design shown on the right, it stated 'It is difficult to understand why one figure should be "new or original" and the other not.' The circumstances of refusal were not made known.

An interesting event occurred when a design application was refused but a later applicant for registration of the same design

APPENDIX G

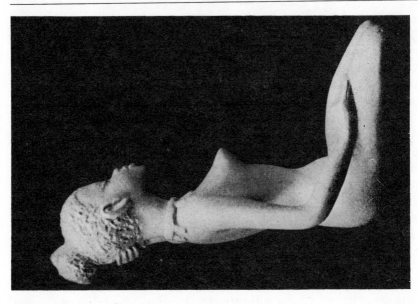

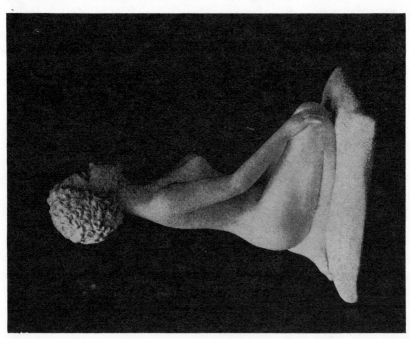

REFUSED

ACCEPTED

Fig. 5.1 Two representations of human figures: (left) application refused;

succeeded in having a similar refusal reversed on appeal. It was held that the earlier application could not be a bar to registration of the later application because refused designs are not officially published and, of course, in this case there was no evidence of prior publication, sale or other use of the first design that had been refused.

Except in the case of secret designs, that were discussed earlier, and designs for specific classes of articles discussed in the next section, the representations or specimens, the application form, the statement of novelty and the Convention documents of registered designs are open to public inspection at the Designs Registry as soon as the registration certificate has been issued, and it is possible to order copies. The register is, of course, also open to inspection.

Only very limited information about registered designs is officially published in print. Such publication as does take place appears in the weekly *Official Journal* (*Patents*). This periodical contains a list of designs that have been registered day by day, giving the name of the registered proprietor, the article in respect of which the design has been registered, the date of registration, and the number. An actual drawing or photograph of the design is not printed, nor is there an entry of any kind concerning designs for textile articles.

5.13 Postponement of publication

The representations or specimens of designs in respect of secret applications cannot be inspected until the secrecy order is lifted (if ever). Further, except by authority of the proprietor, the Registrar or the court, publication of wallpaper and lace designs is postponed for two years from the issue date of the registration certificate and of textile designs for three years but, if the design is being cited by the Registrar as a ground for refusing a subsequent application, the applicant may see the representations or specimens in the presence of the Registrar or one of his officers.

5.15 Searches

Design registrations are not officially published in print for distribution to British and foreign libraries and for classification according to subject matter. File copies of the designs for which there is no bar to publication can, of course, be inspected at the

Designs Registry and copies ordered but for this one must be aware of the existence and number of a prior registration. If only the name of a registered proprietor is known, all the designs owned by him can be found by means of a name search in a card index available at the Registry and then each registration can be inspected upon payment of a fee until the design of particular interest is found. It is impossible for the public to carry out a general review of prior registrations for specific articles and thus it will be evident that a novelty or infringement search amongst registered designs can also not be carried out by the public.

Provision is therefore made for limited searches to be carried out by officers of the Designs Registry upon payment of a fee. An illustration or sample of the article has to be lodged in duplicate with the search request and, depending on which of two forms is filed, the Registrar will advise either whether the design of the article has been registered and is still in force (this search, which goes back about 20 years, is really only suitable for discovering if a specific design is registered) or whether the design or a closely resembling design is currently registered (this search goes back only 15 years and is more suitable for ascertaining infringement and possibly for obtaining an indication of the registrability of a design, but the search is by no means exhaustive in this latter respect since it is limited to design registrations that are still in force). It is to be noted that neither of these official searches is a novelty search.

5.15   Marking of articles

In the UK it is not compulsory to mark articles with some reference to the registration of its design. However, marking is highly desirable from the point of view of claiming damages in infringement proceedings. The preferred form of marking is 'Registered Design No . . .' or any abbreviation of this where space is limited, provided that the number is quoted in full. Without the number, marking has little value, except perhaps for prestige purposes. Well known abbreviations of the marking are 'Reg. Des. No.' and 'R.D.No.' The use of a capital letter 'R' in a circle is meaningless in the UK both from a legal and practical point of view and even abroad it has significance only in connection with a registered trade mark. If the marking cannot be applied to the article itself, it should at least appear on the packaging, catalogues, etc. Products intended for export should be marked with the numbers of the foreign design registrations (if any). In some countries marking is not only advisable but actually compulsory. Vague statements like 'World Designs Pending' or 'British and Foreign Designs' or 'Design registered in the UK and abroad' are quite useless and in some countries illegal if no registration exists. There is no really suitable alternative to the marking of articles in the recommended manner. The registered proprietor could insert a general advertisement in the relevant trade press to announce that the design is registered. This method is often employed abroad but is less certain in its effect and should, at least in the UK, be used with caution to ensure that no particular person or identifiable group of persons is threatened by the advertisement.

5.16 False representation

For falsely representing that a design is registered in the UK in respect of an article sold by him, a person is liable to a fine. False representation in this respect includes wrongful marking of articles with the word 'registered' or any other word suggesting the same thing if there is in fact no design registration, or if there was one but it has expired. Manufacturers should therefore be careful to remove reference to the design registration from articles sold after the registration has expired. Similarly, use of the word 'registered' must be postponed until after a design application has been registered. It should be noted that the false marking of goods is also regulated by the Trade Descriptions Act 1968.

5.17 Compulsory licence

There are two forms of compulsory licence. First, a government department or a person authorized by it may use a registered design for the services of the Crown on terms as agreed between the department and the registered proprietor or as decided by the court. Second, and the rest of this section will be confined to this form, at any time after registration of a design, an interested person may apply to the Registrar for a compulsory licence on the ground that the design is not, in the UK, being industrially applied to a reasonable extent to the article in respect of which it is registered. As in cancellation proceedings, the Registrar has power to award costs, witnesses may be cross-examined and the procedure takes the form of statement, counterstatement, evidence, counter-evidence, evidence in reply and a hearing.

At one time, the only remedy for non-manufacture in the UK was cancellation of the registration. In one reported case, a further six months was allowed to commence adequate working because a delay of six to eight months that had already taken place since registration of the design was not thought to be fatal to the proprietor's rights. In another case, cancellation was ordered because working was solely by importation, there was no obstacle to local manufacture and the proprietor had taken no steps towards manufacture in the UK during the 11 months following registration. In a third case, brought at a time when the ground of non-manufacture could no longer result in cancellation but only in a compulsory licence, it was held that, since the requested grant of a 'licence to import', would not achieve the object of the Act, which was to ensure UK manufacture, a licence would be refused. The only guidance to be had from these three cases is that the registered proprietor is expected to exploit his registration in this country within a matter of months but that a compulsory licence is unlikely to be granted unless the applicant can show that he will work the design principally by local manufacture.

Compulsory licence applications that have been filed under the existing Designs Act have not been prosecuted to a conclusion and remain unreported but the author has been involved in opposing one of these and is of the opinion that nowadays it would be nigh impossible to obtain a compulsory licence under a design registration or, if the Registrar were to decide to grant such a licence, that it would be useless. This is because a compulsory licence could hardly extend to the artistic copyright in the design (as copyright law does not provide for compulsory licensing). Accordingly, in sharp contrast with patents, there is little prospect of compulsory licences being granted for registered designs unless the entire law affecting designs and artistic copyright undergoes a change. Nevertheless, design proprietors who do not wish to be faced even with an abortive application for a compulsory licence should exploit their designs with the minimum of delay.

5.18   Threats

It is illegal to threaten someone with design infringement proceedings. The aggrieved party may bring an action against the offender who, unless he can show that the threats were justified, will be restrained by a court injunction from repeating the threats. The aggrieved party can also recover damages from the offender. The threats need not be in writing to be offensive.

The reason behind these provisions is obvious. A man cannot be expected to carry on business with the cloud of legal proceedings hanging over his head. The person issuing the threats should either start infringement proceedings and have the dispute settled by the court or the threatened party should be able to bring matters to a head by starting an action to restrain threats—the usual turn of events then being that the offender will counter claim for infringement and the threatened party will dispute the validity of the design. In other words, the threatened party will be responsible for initiating the infringement action to obtain a decision one way or the other and enable him to plan his future production or selling programme. He will also have the tactical advantage of being the plaintiff in the action.

A mere notification of the existence of a design registration is not an actionable threat; nor is a general notice warning infringers to beware (unless it is shown that the notice is in reality addressed to a particular person).

The threats provisions are often contravened through ignorance, despite the existence of similar provisions in patent law, but ignorance is not a defence to a threats action. Even professional advisers, not realizing that the threatened party can take countermeasures, have been known to make themselves personally liable by issuing groundless threats on behalf of a client in the hope that the threatened party will be bluffed into submission. The damage resulting to the aggrieved party can be considerable, especially if existing or potential customers have been intimidated by the threats.

5.19 How not to threaten and incense

Assuming that a proprietor has good reason for believing that his design registration is being infringed by a trade rival, it is understandable that he will feel aggrieved and desire to take prompt and stern action to enforce his rights. There is, of course, nothing to stop him from doing so. He can speedily instruct his solicitor to issue a writ and then try to wring satisfaction from the offending party. At this stage neither he nor his solicitor need be concerned with the prohibition against threats because there is no longer any threatening—the writ for infringement has already been issued and perhaps even served. However, it is just as foolish to rush blindly into an infringement action as it is to write threatening letters. For one thing, infringement actions are expensive. The offender may turn out to be stronger from a financial point of view and be prepared to put up a staunch fight. After the heat of the moment has worn off, the design proprietor may therefore have second thoughts about taking hasty action against a formidable opponent. Conversely, the infringer may be financially insecure and not able to pay the costs and damages awarded against him if he loses; perhaps he is not even in a position to compete commercially with the design proprietor and does not therefore constitute a serious threat to his business. For another thing, the infringer may have just cause for ignoring the design registration because he knows it to be invalid.

Accordingly, it is often wise to write a non-threatening warning letter to see what arguments the infringer may have up his sleeve, and to allow the situation to be weighed up by the professional adviser. Such a letter, to be sent by recorded delivery, should draw attention to the proprietor's products of which the design is protected by the registration, which should be identified. Copies of the design representations should preferably be enclosed to save time. The letter may continue that the competitor's advertised articles and/or articles as sold have come to the writer's attention and these would appear closely to resemble the products in which the proprietor enjoys design rights. Finally, the letter can state that the recipient is requested to compare his articles with the enclosed representations and notify his comments within a specified reasonable number of days. Ideally, such a warning letter should say little more. To avoid threats, there must certainly be no hint as to what might happen if the letter is ignored and, to obtain satisfaction, unfriendly language should be avoided. A friendly approach may lead to an amicable solution.

From a commercial point of view, it is important that warning letters be addressed to the real source of annoyance. Except in unusual circumstances, little would be gained by writing to a retailer because he is, after all, a potential customer of the design proprietor himself. The retailer may, however, need to be approached if there is no other way of establishing the identity of the British manufacturer or importer of the offending articles.

5.20 Infringement

Inevitably, many of the previous sections in this book have already made reference to questions appertaining to infringement and relevant portions will not be repeated in detail. The sections concerning novelty are also of interest because the considerations involved in determining novelty are much the same as for infringement.

The competent court for infringement proceedings is the High Court, or the Court of Session in the case of Scotland.

The rights accruing from a design registration have already been enumerated and any or all of these rights can obviously be enforced against infringers. Copying is not a criterion in design infringement considerations; independently conceived similar designs also contravene the rights of the registered proprietor. For an infringement action to be successful, evidence must be produced showing that the offence(s) complained of occurred in the UK (whether the goods were intended for export only does not affect the issue), that the offending article is one to which the design registration extends and that the design of the offending article is substantially the same as that which is registered. The first two of these conditions should usually not prove difficult to determine. The third condition requires comment but it must again be emphasized that the reader should seek help from experts if he suspects infringement of his design or fears that he might infringe someone else's design.

5.21 Substantially the same design

'In fact, I have hitherto never found, in a really contested case relating to designs, so clear a case of infringement.' These words were spoken by a High Court judge in 1896 when holding that the lace design at the left in Fig. 5.2 was infringed by the design at the right. The considerations applied by the courts almost 80 years later are still much the same.

In comparing the registered design with the alleged infringement, the eye is the only judge. If the overall appearance is the same, there is infringement. The representations or specimens on file at the Designs Registry should primarily be used for the comparison rather than the article sold by the registered proprietor. The designs should be compared not only side by side but also at a distance and at different times. The comparison also depends on the mental picture carried away by the person who, having seen an article to which the design has been applied and on seeing another article, will pose himself the question: 'Have I seen that design before or is it something different?'.

REPORTS OF PATENT, DESIGN,   [Sept. 2, 1896.

Oliver and Co. v. Thornley and Co.

IN THE HIGH COURT OF JUSTICE.—CHANCERY DIVISION.

Before MR. JUSTICE ROMER.—July 6th and 7th, 1896.

OLIVER AND CO. *v.* THORNLEY AND CO.

Design.—Action for infringement.—Infringement found.—Form of Order.
This was an action for infringement of a registered design for lace. *The* 5
Defendants did not say that the Plaintiffs' design was not new and original,
but they alleged that, by reason of the publication of other lace designs, the
Plaintiffs' design could not be widely construed and held to cover the design of
the Defendants' lace.
Held, on a comparison of the two designs, that the Defendants' design was a 10
clear infringement.
Order made for an injunction, with costs (setting off any costs incurred on
account of a claim by the Plaintiffs to a narrow width of lace, which was
abandoned), and a penalty of 10l., the Defendants undertaking to deliver up all
infringing lace. 15
On the 4th of July 1895, Messrs. *Thomas Oliver and Son* registered a design
for lace in Class 9, under No. 257,429, of which a picture is given below.

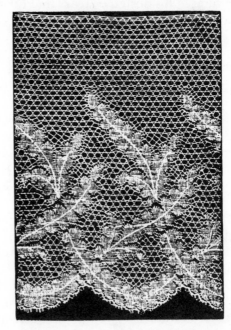

On the 28th of October 1895, Messrs. *Oliver and Co.* commenced an action
against Messrs. *Thornley and Co.* and Messrs. *J. Cox and Co.*, to restrain

Fig. 5.2 First two pages of report on lace designs: (left) design as registered;
(right) infringing design

Oliver and Co. v. *Thornley and Co.*

infringement of this design, claiming damages or profits, delivery up of infringements, and penalties.

Messrs. *Thornley and Co.* had ordered Messrs. *J. Cox and Co.* to prepare lace for them, a picture of which is here given.

5   On the 29th of November 1895, an Order was made on a motion, *J. Cox and Co.* consenting, that *J. Cox and Co.* be thereby perpetually restrained from applying or causing to be applied, or manufacturing or selling, lace made in infringement of the Plaintiffs' registered design ; and further proceedings were stayed against *J. Cox and Co.* ; and the Plaintiffs undertaking to abide by any
10   order as to damages, and the Defendants *Thornley and Co.* undertaking not to sell any patterns of the lace alleged to be an infringement, no Order was made against them.

By consent, the action was set down for trial without pleadings, the Defendants to deliver to the Plaintiffs, on or before the 11th of January 1896,
15   Particulars of alleged anticipations and patterns of the lace to be relied on at the trial.

The following Particulars were delivered on the 22nd of February 1896 by the Defendants *Thornley and Co.* :—The Defendants allege that they have not infringed the Plaintiffs' design. The Defendants do not allege that the
20   Plaintiffs' design is not a new and original design, but they allege that by reason of the publication of the following lace designs prior to the registration of the Plaintiffs' design, that design cannot be construed too widely and held to cover the design of the lace manufactured by Defendants, which is a new and original design :—(*a*) Two lace patterns designed by *William Selby*, of
25   Nottingham, in 1863 ; (*b*) a lace pattern manufactured by Messrs. *Heymann and Co.*, of Nottingham, in May 1895 ; (*c*) a lace pattern manufactured by *H. W. Bircumshaw*, of Nottingham, in 1892 ; (*d*) a lace pattern manufactured in 1885 ; (*e*) seven lace patterns manufactured by the Defendant *Joseph Thornley* in 1882, 1884, 1890, and 1893, patterns of which are contained in the said
30   Defendant's pattern book ; (*f*) the lace patterns Nos. 8, 9, and 10 on marked pages of a pattern book in the Defendant *J. Thornley's* possession, being

Of whose eyes are we speaking here: the court's, the design expert's, a man's in the street, the manufacturer's, the retailer's or the purchaser's? As explained in section 2.10, the point is settled in connection with assessing the registrability of a design, for which purpose the eyes of the customer are decisive. The point is not yet settled for assessing novelty (section 2.21) but, again, the court will probably consider the question through the eyes of the customer. In infringement considerations, it is also likely to be the customers' eyes that will be regarded decisive. In 1973, Lord Justice Russel delivering judgment in the Court of Appeal in an infringement action on the design for a stacking chair stated:

> As we see it, our task is to look at these two chairs, to observe their similarities and differences, to see them together and separately, and to bear in mind that in the end the question whether or not the design of the defendant's chair is substantially different from that of the plaintiff is to be answered by consideration of the respective designs as a whole; and apparently, although we do not think it affects our present decision, viewed as though through the eyes of a consumer or customer.

These comments are not really surprising because in a 1925 case concerning wallpaper designs the judge, after pointing out that it was impossible to distinguish the one design from the other when viewed side by side or at a distance or at different times, went on to say 'I am not referring to those persons who are experts in the trade; it would appear likely that this custom of making followers has taught those experts readily to look for and to distinguish comparatively small differences between two designs. I am thinking of the public, and it is against confusion by the public that the plaintiffs are as much entitled to be protected as confusion in the trade.'

Consequently, regard must be had to the customer's eye.

In an infringement action of a registered design for a lavatory cistern, it was established that the feature of tapering one or both pairs of sides of the water tank was common to the trade, that, when made of cast iron, the tank and lid needed to be thickened at the mouth for manufacturing reasons (and this was usually done by means of an external flange) and that, when made of earthenware, irregularities in manufacture prevented an accurate fit being obtained between the tank and lid and therefore the lid was deliberately designed to exhibit an overhang to disguise the defect. The cistern of the registered design was smoothly contoured, having tapered and bowed tank sides, except the back which was flat, a lid that was domed both longitudinally and transversely, and a semi-circular bead at the junction between the tank and the lid. The judge had no doubt whatever that these features (other than the flat back) of the registered design were new over various illustrations and samples. The allegedly infringing cistern showed 'plain differentiation' in plan, front elevation and side elevation. Nevertheless, the judge commented:

> On the other hand, when the perspective views are examined (and particularly if repeated observation is made of the alleged infringement at substantial time intervals) the differentiation to which I have referred and which is so plainly observable in the plan, front and side views, becomes merged in a resemblence which to my eye is quite inescapable, and which makes the distinction between these articles to me possible only by a determined and conscious mental effort.

Infringement was found.

Slight variations do not avoid design infringement; even extensive variations in detail can still result in a design having the same overall appearance. In comparing his design with a registered design, the manufacturer must therefore beware of falling into the trap of paying too much attention to differences in detail. This was the moral to be drawn from an Appeal Court decision when reversing a High Court judgment in the case of a stove which the defendants had admittedly copied but, so they thought, made a sufficient number of departures to steer clear of the proprietor's rights. The Court of Appeal considered the case in the following manner. They placed the designs side by side, listed the features which the designs had in common, found that these common features constituted a tolerably adequate description of the registered design as well as of the allegedly infringing design, and finally ascertained that this description was not applicable to any form of stove known before the date of the design registration. Infringement was found and one of the appeal judges specifically mentioned that the design consists of the whole thing in the proportion of parts; being able to point to a particular part or parts (for example, a window in the stove) and show that the differences are manifest does not answer the allegation that the one design is the same as the other; the defendants took all the essential elements of the plaintiffs' design. Another of the appeal judges said that had he ordered the plaintiffs' stove in a shop but received delivery of the defendants' stove, he should not have had the slightest idea that he had received the wrong one. The dissimilarity in detail was not such that one could remember.

Time and again infringers have tried to argue that because their designs showed differences from the representations of the registrations, infringement had been avoided; and time and again the courts have pointed out that it is the essential features which matter, not the differences in detail. In an infringement where the novelty of a registered lace design was not in dispute, the judge said: 'No doubt there are differences between them which are apparent when the two are put together and carefully examined; but the essential features of the plaintiffs are taken; and the differences, which are differences of detail, do not prevent the two designs from being essentially the same.'

The courts are tending to give a wide interpretation to some designs. Size is immaterial in determining infringement but the relative proportions might make a considerable difference. Manufacture or sale of a flexible figure having the same characteristic features as those illustrated in the registration is probably sufficient to establish infringement regardless of whether the figures can be manipulated into exactly the same attitude as that chosen for the representations of the registration. Articles registered as a set are protected individually.

5.22 Effect of novelty claims and disclaimers

If the statement of novelty highlights certain features, correspondingly greater attention should be paid to them. Similarly, any disclaimer in the statement of novelty should be noted. It is established that a design must be regarded *in toto*, i.e., when the article is viewed as a whole, and that parts of articles are not registrable alone. A statement of novelty, the purpose of which is simply to place emphasis on the novelty of, or to disclaim novelty in, certain design features, can therefore never have the effect of compelling the court to ignore the unclaimed or disclaimed features completely because disregarding some parts is contrary to considering the design as a whole and would amount to granting protection for only the other parts. Nevertheless, it is true to say that in infringement proceedings a judge will first look at the features that are claimed (or not disclaimed) and if those features have not been taken by the defendant then the judge will not pay very much attention to the rest; if they have been taken, he is bound to consider the rest because they could very well affect the appearance of the article as a whole.

5.23 Effect of prior art

One should try to find the essence of the design, i.e., what the essential or striking features of the registered design are, and then see whether these are incorporated in the offending design and whether any differences that are evident are substantial. As already stated, the considerations involved in this respect are not unlike those applied in determining the novelty of a registrable design over the prior art. On the face of it, the test for infringement is not strictly the same as the test for novelty. To constitute an infringement, a design must be identical with, or not substantially different from, the registered design. To be novel, the design should differ from the prior art in more than just immaterial details. It has been argued that the different wording used in the Act for infringement and novelty considerations makes it easier to establish infringement of a design than it does to invalidate a design. The court has rejected this contention and ruled that the tests for infringement and novelty are the same in practice.

The prior art should also be taken into account when determining infringement, especially when the differences between the alleged infringement and the registered design are not major ones. If the novelty in the registered design is substantial then the protection afforded by the design is also substantial and very considerable changes would need to be made by a competitor before he can be sure of having avoided infringement but, if only small differences distinguish the registered design from prior designs, small differences will similarly suffice to escape infringement of the registration. Where the allegedly infringing design resembles an old design more than it does the registered design, there is unlikely to be infringement. Going one step further, where the differentiating feature between the registered design and what has gone before is not evident in the allegedly infringing design, there can be no infringement, no matter how great the resemblance may be in other respects. Thus, if the registered design of a bottle is old except in respect of a twisted neck, the proprietor can obviously not prevent others from making and selling bottles without twisted necks. The registered design for an oil can for cyclists was once found to be old except for rounded top and bottom edges. A competitor who made oil cans with sharp edges therefore did not infringe. When the registered design qualified for registration by being original in so far that some known subject had been applied to an article, then the better known the subject, the more closely will a competitor's design have to resemble the registered design before it constitutes an infringement.

5.24   Further decided infringement actions

To demonstrate the practical result of applying the previously described principles and tests of infringement, the reader may find it helpful to consider the following few decisions taken at random from decided cases in which the reports included illustrations.

(a) Figure 5.3 shows a registered design for a cup and plate rack and Figs. 5.4, 5.5 and 5.6 show reproductions prepared from photographs of the defendants' rack. These photographs were not actually before the court, but, of course, the rack itself was. The novelty of the registered design was put in dispute. The judge, when referring to two citations (prior designs), said:

> It is an interesting characteristic of both (being embodiments of another's conception of a wire cup and plate rack) that the constituent wires forming the article are all of the same cross-sectional area. It is a striking characteristic, as I see it, of the plaintiffs' design that that conception was departed from, and no one can observe the design and examine the embodiment without being struck by the effect upon the eye which is created by the disparity in size between those parts of the construction which form the main frame and those portions corresponding to the slats or dividing members which form both the base of the two tiers and the back of the device. That is a most striking characteristic, and it is, to my eye, perhaps the main design feature in the sense of the initial feature to impress itself upon the mind.
>
> I find no difficulty whatever in coming to the conclusion that this is a novel and original design constituting a sufficient departure from the prior art as to justify registration as a valid design, and accordingly on that part of the case the plaintiffs have satisfied me that they are entitled to the benefit of the statutory monopoly which is conferred on registration under the Registered Designs Act.

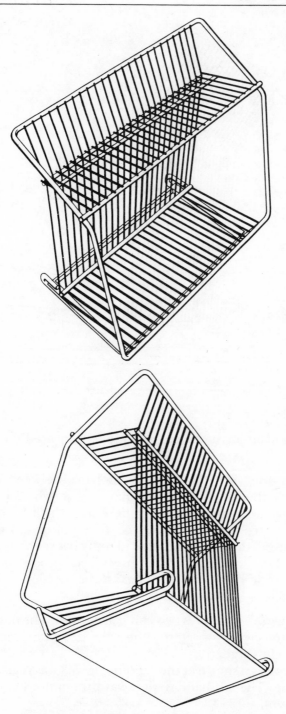

Fig. 5.3 Cup and plate rack design registration

Fig. 5.4   Cup and plate rack of infringing design (*see also* Figs. 5.5 and 5.6)

In pronouncing infringement, the judge later used the following words:

> I take the view that the resemblance between these two designs, the details of which I have not sought to enumerate, are such as to outweigh the differences which I have been at pains to try and point out, and I cannot myself escape the conclusion that the substantial identity between the designs of these two articles would impress itself upon those whose business or interest brings them into connection with this type of article.

(b) Figure 5.7 illustrates two golf ball designs. The design on the left was protected by a registration. The design on the right was held not to infringe.

(c) The design shown at the right in Fig. 5.8 was registered for a slipper case. The left-hand design was pronounced to be clear of infringement.

Fig. 5.5 Cup and plate rack of infringing design

Fig. 5.6 Cup and plate rack of infringing design

(d) Figure 5.9 shows a design for a table lamp as registered by the plaintiff. The designs of Figs. 5.10 and 5.11 were subsequently registered in the name of the defendant. The history of the lamps was an interesting one. The defendant had bought a prototype lamp of the registered design from a person who knew that the prototype was not his to sell because it belonged to the plaintiff. The disclosure of the design by prior sale was therefore held to be a breach of trust and could not be used to invalidate the plaintiff's registration. The court held further that the plaintiff's registration had been infringed not only by lamps substantially the same as that of Fig. 5.9 but also by a modified lamp that looked practically the same as that in Fig. 5.10. The Fig. 5.10 registration was ordered to be expunged by reason of prior registration of the Fig. 5.9 design. The defendant's registration as shown in Fig. 5.11 was declared valid at the trial but invalid by the Court of Appeal.

The Court of Appeal explained that it was significant that a foul anchor and a cabin lamp made into a table lamp was broadly novel.

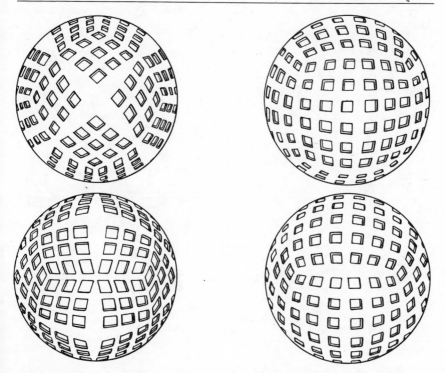

Fig. 5.7 Golf ball designs: (left) design registered; (right) design held not to infringe

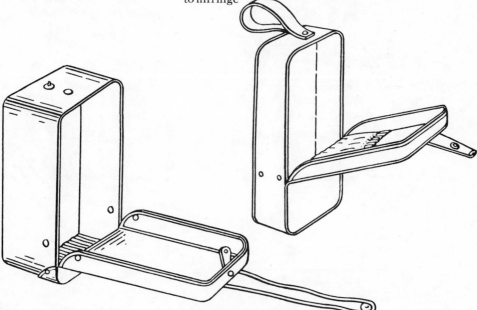

Fig. 5.8 Slipper case designs: (right) design as registered; (left) design held not to infringe

Fig. 5.9   Registered table lamp design

Fig. 5.10   Table lamp according to infringing design

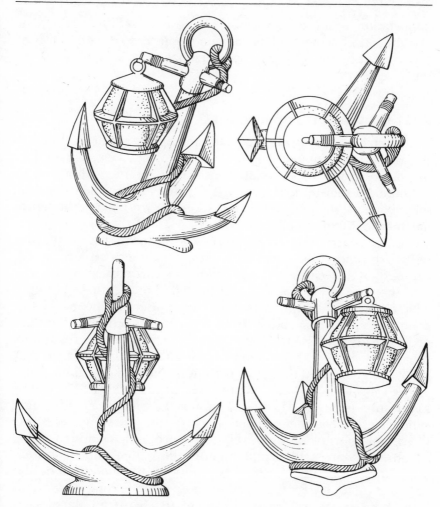

Fig. 5.11 Defendant's table lamp; registration expunged on appeal

Judged by the eye, said the Appeal Court, the trial judge rightly held that the differences between the designs were no more than variations on an essential theme.

5.25 Infringements that are not actionable

Any infringement committed before the date on which the certificate of registration issued is not actionable; nor is anything done outside the United Kingdom of Great Britain, Northern Ireland and the Isle of Man and the same applies to manufacture or importation other than for the purpose of selling, trading or carrying on a business. Thus, making a registered design by way of experiment or for testing or for personal use does not constitute infringement.

5.26   Contributory infringement

The doctrine of contributory infringement does not exist in UK design law (or, for that matter, in UK patent law). Unless two persons or companies actually conspire or collude with a view to infringing a registered design, the writ for infringement must be served against the person who is responsible for making the article having the infringing design.

Assume that a design is registered for a garden seat made from peculiarly shaped battens and having ornate legs on a frame. A competitor A decides to market a similar garden seat having the same battens and legs as those illustrated in the registered design. The competitor is not a manufacturer himself; he purchases components for his product from other manufacturers. Thus, he orders ready-for-assembly battens from supplier B and ready-for-assembly frames with legs from supplier C. It will be recalled that the right given by a design registration is to make or import the article for sale or for business purposes, or to market it. The article in question is that to which the registered design or a confusingly similar design has been applied. Accordingly, the suppliers B and C are not contravening the registered proprietor's design rights because they are neither making nor selling the complete garden seat. The competitor A would be guilty of infringing the design registration if he were to assemble seats from the components and offer them for sale or hire but he decides to sell instead a kit of parts for assembly by the purchaser. This is unlikely to be an infringing act for which he can be sued under the Registered Designs Act. He may possibly be falling foul of the Copyright Act (discussed later in this book) but he has escaped design infringement. The persons buying and assembling the kit of parts will for the most part be householders requiring the seats for their personal use, so even they are not infringing the design registration. (The position would be different if manufacturers B and C act in concert in the knowledge that when their respective components are put together the resulting garden seat infringes someone's design rights.)

The reader might say that the manufacturing suppliers should be liable because one of the rights accruing from registration is to prevent others from making anything that enables an infringing article to be made. Unfortunately, parts of articles (in this case the components for the seat) are not something enabling an article to be made. A printing roller for applying textile designs, a mould for forming plastics articles or a die for extruding metal articles would all be something enabling infringing articles to be made, but not so the components of the articles themselves.

The plaintiffs in a real case that came to trial were the owners of three designs registered for children's tricycles. The predominant feature of each design was the inclusion of a boot between the rear wheels. The defendants made and sold somewhat similar boots with instructions for fitting to existing tricycles. The judge held that a part of the whole article to which the registered design is applied is not something that enables the article to be made (this was confirmed in *Dorling v. Honnor Marine*, discussed in chapter 7 on copyright).

5.27 The litigation

A licensee who is recorded as such on the register may be joined with the registered proprietor as co-plaintiff in an infringement action. The Act does not confer power on an exclusive licensee to sue infringers in his own name. This is another aspect where design law differs from patent law. If the registered proprietor of a lace design sells his lace in an incomplete state to a second party—a firm of lace finishers who also have the exclusive right to sell the finished lace—it is still only the registered proprietor who can bring the action. The finishers have no cause of action, either alone or jointly with the proprietor. The position would be different, of course, if the finishers are co-proprietors of the registration.

The defendant may be the workman who was responsible for applying the infringing design to an article, or his employer, or an importer or a salesman, and so on.

The mechanics of bringing an infringement action can be summarized as below.

(a) Plaintiff obtains proof of infringement (such as by making an invoiced purchase of the infringing article).
(b) The writ is issued.
(c) At this stage there may be a series of letters, written 'without prejudice' to the outcome of the action if brought to court, with a view to reaching a settlement.

(d) The writ is served on the defendant.

(e) The defendant enters an appearance (if he is still intent on contesting the action).

(f) The plaintiff lodges his statement of claim and particulars of the infringing actions.

(g) The defendant presents his defence, including any counter-claim, and particulars of objections.

(h) The plaintiff serves his reply, including his defence to any counterclaim, on the defendant.

(i) The plaintiff and defendant write to each other to ask and answer whether any admissions are being made.

(j) Summons are taken out by the plaintiff or, in default, by the defendant for directions concerning the trial and possibly directions for further and better pleadings or particulars.

(k) Finally, the case is set down for trial in the court, but at any time up to and including the trial the parties may agree to settle their differences, possibly with the approval of the court.

In the High Court, design cases are invariably tried by one of two judges who are experienced in industrial property matters. The trial judge's decision is subject to appeal, the court of second instance being the Court of Appeal which is composed of three appeal judges. Very rarely, design cases go to the third instance, namely the House of Lords, where the case will be heard by five Law Lords. In all instances, each party will be represented by a specialist solicitor who is briefed by the design agent and who, in turn, briefs a barrister. There are several barristers who are expert in design matters. Apart from advising his client (through the solicitor) during all stages of the proceedings, the barrister pleads the case in the court. In important cases, it is not uncommon for a party to engage two barristers—a junior counsel and a leading counsel. Of course, the plaintiff or defendant may argue his own case but the foolishness of doing this will be self-evident.

It may be mentioned that interlocutory injunctions (court orders preventing the defendant from continuing with the act com-plained of until the case comes to trial) are so difficult to obtain that they are rarely sought, especially if the registration is a recent one and its validity is disputed by the defendant.

Legal aid may be obtainable by a defendant or plaintiff in an infringement action but it is difficult to qualify for this. Informa-tion in this respect is obtainable from the Law Society. Legally aided cases are most rare in the field of intellectual or industrial property. The author knows of only two such cases. One concerned an appeal in a patent infringement action, the other a manufacturer of wall plaques who went to the Court of Appeal in a design case. One would not normally know whether or not a litigant has obtained legal aid but in the design case a practice question arose in relation to a proposed order for costs and was reported.

5.28 Innocent infringer

Innocence is not a defence to infringement proceedings; an injunction will still be granted but an infringer who can prove that he was not aware, and had no reasonable ground for supposing, that the design was registered is not liable for damages, notwithstanding the fact that the design proprietor's articles are vaguely marked 'registered' without including the number of the registration. If the preferred form of marking is employed, this will help, but even then there is no guarantee that damages will be awarded against the infringer as part of the relief. Theoretically, an infringer could nevertheless prove that he had no reasonable ground to suppose that the design registration existed—for example, if the infringer had no opportunity of seeing the proprietor's articles or design. Again, the infringer may have been fully aware of the design registration but availed himself of the design at a time when he believed the registration had already ceased because the renewal fee had not been paid, and was not paid until later. In practice, innocence is difficult to establish; a wise design proprietor will have brought the registration to the infringer's notice at a very early date.

5.29 To sue or not to sue?

Infringement actions are expensive to pursue in this country. There are many preliminaries and the expenses of the hearing itself. £1500 per day of hearing is not an overestimate but one never knows what to expect when one first embarks on litigation. In contrast, in certain other countries, such as Germany, a monetary value is put on the infringing act in dispute and the legal fees, including the court costs, are a set percentage of this value and recoverable from the loser. The first question that the UK design proprietor should therefore ask himself is whether he can afford to fight a court case. If he wins and the court awards costs in his favour, he cannot expect to recoup all of his actual expenses by any means. Second, if the defendant is ordered to pay damages (which could be the subject of a separate inquiry), the plaintiff might only recover his loss of profits or a payment equivalent to the royalty that the infringer would have paid had he been a legitimate licensee; does the likely financial compensation outweigh the time, trouble and anxiety of a court action and the out-of-pocket expenses? Third, what is the financial standing of the infringer? Does he have the capital to pay the costs and damages that one hopes will be awarded against him or will he simply go bankrupt (or into liquidation in the case of a company) and leave the plaintiff holding the baby?

Except in cases of persistent plagiarism where a competitor habitually encroaches on a registered proprietor's rights and must be taught a lesson once and for all (such cases do arise in practice and have been successfully pursued by the author), it is better by far to reach an amicable agreement soon after the writ for infringement has been issued. It may not be possible to extract the same satisfaction from an infringer in an out-of-court settlement, but it is more sensible. One should be able to negotiate a royalty payment in respect of past infringement, a contribution towards the legal costs, an enforcible undertaking to respect the design registration in future and delivery up or destruction of unsold stocks and tools for applying the protected design.

5.30 Damages

The design proprietor is entitled to recover the damage occasioned by the infringer's offers for sale and actual sales of the infringing articles. One should consider the situation that the plaintiff would have been in had the defendant not acted contrary to the plaintiff's rights and the damages should seek to restore that situation; but punitive damages are out of the question. In the hot-water bottle case discussed previously, a subsequent inquiry as to damages reached the High Court some two years after the date of judgment because the parties were unable to agree a fair basis for damages and wished to obtain directions from the court. It had been established that about half a million bottles were sold by the defendants. If the plaintiffs would have had a non-exclusive licence, they could have been made to pay the same royalty for the half million infringing hot-water bottles as other licensees were in the habit of paying. But there was no other licensee, so an alternative measure for assessing damages had to be found. The judge took into account that the defendants' action in continuing to sell the infringing bottles for about five years after becoming aware of the design registration in suit implied that they were procuring the important commercial benefits of the design for their sales. The fact that the defendants changed to a commercially successful alternative design after judgment did not alter the pre-judgment position, which alone is relevant to an inquiry as to damages. Also, it had to be considered whether the defendants' sales would otherwise have enured to the benefit of the plaintiffs, taking into account any peculiar circumstances of the defendants' business that created outlets not available to other traders.

Other factors that might be pertinent to an assessment of the amount of damages are any special skills and advantages possessed by the infringer; if he has an old established business; the goodwill of the defendants' customers; the effect the infringements might have had on the plaintiffs' future sales (e.g., the defendants might have exhausted the market).

Damages in design infringement proceedings must not be confused with fines imposed on a wrongdoer as a form of punishment. Also, damages should not have the effect of putting the plaintiffs in a better position than if the infringement of his rights had not taken place at all. Finally, no award of damages is made in respect of infringements that took place more than six years before the issue of the writ.

5.31 Liquidated companies

An occasion may arise where a manufacturer desires to use a design for which a registration is owned by a company that has in the meantime gone into liquidation, without the liquidator realizing that all the assets of the company have not been disposed of. In such an event, the manufacturer could seek cancellation of the registration or rectification of the register on the ground that the proprietor has ceased to exist. A better and probably cheaper course is to negotiate to purchase the registration. If a company has been finally wound up and some undisposed property of the company is subsequently discovered, this property belongs to the Treasury and the Treasury Solicitor may dispose of the property as he deems best. It might under these circumstances be possible to purchase the design registration from the Treasury for a small sum, say £50, if there is no other bidder.

5.32   Costs and value of design registration

The cost of obtaining and maintaining a design registration is variable. At the time of writing, the UK government filing fee, including registration for the first five years, was £21 for a single article (reduced to £5 for a lace, check or stripe design) and £42 (reduced to £10) for a set of articles. All designs cost £52 to renew for the second five year period and £74 for the third and final five year period. In contrast with patent law, there is no provision for 'licences of right' endorsements that might halve the renewal fees. Nor is there assistance for the poor, as exists in some other countries.

The government fees are, of course, not the only expenses involved. Assuming that the applicant is represented by an agent, one must add the agent's service charge; alternatively, the applicant should add the cost of his own time and effort for obtaining appropriate forms, preparing the application papers, instructing a draughtsman, and diarizing the renewal dates. Then there is the actual out-of-pocket expense for the formal drawings or photographs. Irrespective of whether an agent is employed, it is unlikely that a simple design registration can be obtained for an initial cost of less than £50.

Is this good value for money? The answer must be an emphatic yes for an applicant who considers it worth his while to hold his competitors at bay—to compel his competitors to do their own creative designing. It must be regarded as decidedly economical to obtain a five year monopoly in the design of a product at a cost of roughly £50.

Another aspect that requires consideration is which product merits the spending of money to obtain a design monopoly. This resolves to strictly commercial considerations. Presumably, substantial thought and effort were expended in creating the design for a product that is to have sales appeal. The manufacturer may say: yes, but I would much prefer to have patent protection so that no one can make my product, no matter what it looks like. This is a valid point but reference to sections 1.7 to 1.10 of this book will show that there are circumstances when a design registration is either the only form of available protection or valuable additional protection. Of course, if one is convinced that there is nothing to gain from a design registration, even £50 will be too much to spend.

Assuming that it has been decided that a design monopoly will be desirable, it must be considered how much profit one expects to make from the product. If a new business is to be built up with the product, the £50 should be regarded as a calculated business risk to be added to the far larger other sums that are being risked in the venture. Where the product represents an additional line in an established business, it is a matter of calculating or estimating the net profit over the first five years. As a rule of thumb, if one cannot hope to clear at least £500 in five years, a design registration is not warranted because it would cost too high a percentage of the profit. £500 in five years amounts to £100 per year—a ludicrously low sum, one may think, in these times when companies are used to spending thousands of pounds just to get a product off the ground. However, it must be borne in mind that we are considering the case where no risk is to be taken, the other expenses in launching the product have already been taken into account and there might be numerous other new or improved products to which the same considerations have to be applied each year. Although only an economist is qualified to provide a reliable calculation, and tax questions are also involved, the author ventures to guess that £500 is the minimum net profit to be anticipated over the first five years to make a design application worthwhile at the present time, and more if and when the cost of obtaining design registrations increases. Similarly, if the product having the registered design is still selling after five and ten years, respectively, there is little sense in paying for renewal fees unless more than £200 net profit is expected in each following year.

The above disregards the somewhat doubtful prestige value of owning a design registration, the existence and number of which one can quote in advertising literature and on the product. If prestige is indeed attached to a design registration, one might as well lump the registration expenses in with the advertising costs.

Design protection in most other countries is costlier to obtain than in the UK—an average of £150 per country in order to get a foreign application on file is an extremely rough guide at the present time. If exports are contemplated to ten or so countries, the possible registration expenses can reach a figure that merits evaluation by a financial consultant (also see section 6.3).

5.33 Commercial exploitation

In common with inventors, a major problem that is very frequently encountered by the authors of designs is how best to commercialize the results of their endeavours. This problem does not, of course, arise with designers who are rewarded by special bonus schemes organized by their employers or whose designing capabilities are reflected in their salaries in cases where the designs belong to the employers by reason of express or implied service contracts.

We are here concerned with the numerous independent designers who have a valuable contribution to make towards the better designing of products but who experience difficulty in finding a suitable opening in industry. A research and development department of a company is understandably jealous of its reputation. An outsider may not meet with an enthusiastic reception from such a department because it fears that the acceptance of a design suggestion from an independent designer is likely to be regarded as an indication of some shortcoming in its own capabilities. The reasoning behind this fear is that the management might consider the development department to be superfluous or lacking in ideas if independent designers can do as well or even better. This attitude is clearly ill founded but it is met time and again. Company executives are more likely to lend a sympathetic ear to an outsider but the top people are difficult to approach, not only because visitors are expected to follow more or less set channels leading to minor executives who make sure that the bosses are not needlessly bothered, but also by reason of a lack of drive and persuasiveness on the part of the designer.

A designer must be prepared to persevere and bear the disappointment of submitting his work to countless companies before any notice is taken of him, unless he is fortunate to possess influential contacts or even financial backers to help him start up his own business. He may eventually have to resort to employing the services of a broker whose business it is to build up a portfolio of designs available for exploitation and a list of companies in various countries looking for new products. The idea is that through experience and established connections the broker finds it easier than the designer to ferret out the right kind of manufacturer for a product and to negotiate the best possible terms. Naturally, the broker expects to be paid for his services and it will therefore cost the design author a percentage of the royalties that are eventually paid by the manufacturer with whom the design is placed. Usually, an initial down payment for expenses is also stipulated by the broker and another requirement might be that all subsequent inquiries received, or contacts made, by the designer must be referred to the broker.

Design registration agents do not normally include exploitation as part of their services, although the author knows some who do and who are therefore in great demand. Most agents prefer to effect introductions between clients and then leave it to the clients to negotiate.

6. *Design registrations abroad*

6.1. Registration procedures in other countries

From what has gone before, it will be evident to the reader that the design law in the UK is complex, even though the procedures for obtaining a registration may be straightforward. It would fill an impossibly large number of pages to describe the often vastly different laws and procedures in other countries that have independent provision for the protection of industrial designs. British law and practice is followed fairly closely in several Commonwealth countries such as Australia and New Zealand, and former Commonwealth countries such as South Africa. The law in countries on the Continent varies extensively. The US has a peculiar design law of its own and the Canadian law is different again, although it stems from the British.

Under US law, inventiveness is required to merit registration and a specification has to be drawn up with a claim in the same way as for patents. This is why the registration is termed a 'design patent'. It is not infringed unless the defendant's article is a fairly close copy, so the benefits of spending a comparatively large sum on filing and prosecuting an application to grant in the US may seem doubtful. This is offset by the far greater 'patent' consciousness and respect for issued design patents shown by US businessmen. In Canada, an accurate description of the design is required in words as well as in pictures. In Japan, the drawing requirements are most curious, pictorial views not being permitted. Germany makes provision for collective design applications (a large number of articles in one and the same application) but infringement of a registration is found only on proof of copying, which brings the design law outside the registration concept as it is understood in the UK and more into the realms of a depositing procedure for

148

copyright. In Nigeria printing blocks of the drawings are called for. A classification system according to the material in which the design is executed is employed for designs in Australia. Even a shortlist of peculiarities in the various countries would take up too much space so, if the reader has practical problems affecting other territories, he should seek professional advice. Design agents in the UK either have personal knowledge of foreign design protection and enforcement, or work in close cooperation with overseas agents and attorneys who will be able to give the necessary guidance.

The following fundamental points are worth mentioning here. Apart from the countries mentioned later, to which a UK design registration extends automatically, a separate application for registration must be filed in each country where protection is desired. Priority can be claimed from the basic British application in most countries (so that the effective foreign filing date will in fact be the British filing date in the reciprocal manner to that described in section 3.14 for foreign designs filed in the UK with a claim to priority from abroad), provided that the foreign application is lodged within six months of the British application. If priority is not claimed, the foreign registration may be invalid by reason of prior publication or prior use or prior registration of the design in the UK; this will vary from country to country. The official requirements are also different in other countries, as are the maximum terms of the resulting registrations and the protection afforded by them. Marking of the product with the registration number is compulsory in some countries and in others wrongful marking is severely punishable as an act of unfair competition. Indeed, exporters should be particularly careful in those countries having a law against unfair competition because it is very easy to contravene such a law by comparative or laudatory statements in advertising literature that would seem harmless in the UK.

6.2 Are foreign nationals more design conscious?

Although, compared with countries such as Argentina, Sweden, Australia, India and the Soviet Union, citizens of the UK not surprisingly make more use of their own national design registration system, it is significant that in, say, the year 1972 there were almost 6000 Koreans who filed design applications in Korea, 11 500 French applicants in France, 54 000 Japanese, 59 000 Germans (Federal Republic) and 4400 Spaniards, but only 3560 UK citizens who filed design applications in the UK. Admittedly, the UK now also provides design protection under copyright law; this may, albeit inadvisably, discourage some design proprietors from making use of the registration procedure. However, the indications are that British manufacturers are not as design conscious as they ought to be.

Another interesting comparison is the extent to which various nationals file foreign design applications. In this respect, UK design owners led the world in 1972, followed by Austria and the Federal Republic of Germany. This indicates that, when finally motivated to become protection conscious, British manufacturers are more prone to seek corresponding foreign design registrations than are most other nationals. Unfortunately, by far the most popular foreign countries to which Britons look for design registration are the Federal Republic of Germany, France and the US—the very countries where registrations are probably less valuable because they afford less protection.

6.3 Where to file abroad

Foreign design registrations are comparatively expensive to obtain. As a rough guide, one must be prepared to pay in each foreign country at least three times the cost of a British registration. This is not only because the government fees are usually higher abroad and the exchange rate works against us but also because it is essential to engage the services of an agent in the country in question (usually through the intermediary of the British design agent). From a practical point of view, it is therefore almost always impossible to file a corresponding design application in every country that has provision for design registrations. A list of these countries is given in Fig. 6.1. Where the British manufacturer has overseas subsidiary or associated companies or distributing agents, some of the countries where he requires design protection are more or less determined for him already, especially if his foreign contacts are prepared to pay the registration costs, and he need then only decide whether an even wider territory is to be covered.

As a first step, a manufacturer should determine the upper limit of what he can afford to spend on foreign design protection without sacrificing a reasonable profit on his sales. Unfortunately, this usually means that the sales of his products in the UK must finance the foreign spending because at the early stage of production planning, when a final decision on foreign filings becomes

Countries in which legislation exists for the registration of designs
(excluding territories to which a UK registration extends automatically)

†African and Malagasy Union (comprising Cameroon, Central African Republic,
 Congo, Dahomey, Gabon, Ivory Coast, Malagasy Republic, Mauritania, Niger,
 Senegal, Tchad Republic, Togo, Upper Volta)
†Algeria
†Argentina
†Australia (including New Guinea, Norfolk Island, Papua)
†Austria
†Bahama Islands
∗Bahrain
 Bangladesh
†Benelux (comprising Belgium, Netherlands, Luxembourg)
†Brazil
†Bulgaria
 Burundi
†Canada
 Channel Islands (see Guernsey, Jersey)
 Chile (for local manufacture only)
 Colombia
†Cuba
†Czechoslovakia
†Denmark
†Finland
†France
 Gaza District
†Germany (Democratic Republic)
†Germany (Federal Republic)
†Ghana
∗Guernsey
†Hungary
 India
†Ireland
†Israel
†Italy
†Japan
∗Jersey
†Jordan
 Korea (South)
 Kuwait
†Lebanon
†Libya
†Liechtenstein
†Malawi
†Mexico
†Monaco
†Morocco (Ex-French Zone)
†Morocco (Tangier Zone)
†New Zealand (including Samoa, Cook Islands, Tokelau Islands)

Fig. 6.1   List of countries in which legislation exists for the registration of designs

†Nigeria
†Norway
 Pakistan
 Panama
 Peru
†Philippines
†Poland
†Portugal (including Azores and Madeira)
†Rhodesia
 Rwanda
 Somali Republic (as applicable to the former Somalia)
†South Africa
 South West Africa
†Spain
†Sri Lanka
†Sweden
†Switzerland
†Syrian Arab Republic
 Taiwan
†Trinidad and Tobago
†Tunisia
†USSR
†United Arab Republic (Egypt)
†United Kingdom of Great Britain, Northern Ireland and the Isle of Man
†USA (including Panama Canal Zone, Puerto Rico, Virgin Islands)
†Uruguay
 Venezuela
 Western Somoa
†Yugoslavia
†Zaire
†Zambia

* Only by validating a UK registration.
† Signatory to the International Convention.

Fig. 6.1   (contd.)

necessary, it is invariably not known whether there will be any foreign sales at all. In some instances, however, there might be a prospective foreign licensee who is prepared to pay something for taking an option and this money can be set aside for the overseas application costs.

Having placed a monetary limit on the foreign design expenses, dividing this figure by £150 will provide a rough guide as to the number of countries the budget will allow. A calculated guess is now necessary as to where the product can be successfully sold. If necessary, the list can be shortened by deleting those countries which are not sufficiently industrialized to make the same product themselves, i.e., the countries where the main competition is expected to arise from imported imitations. This is not to say that registrations are superfluous in these countries—on the contrary, a registration will be useful in keeping out infringing imports—but non-industrialized countries might have to be disregarded for financial reasons. On the other hand, the list should preferably be augmented by including those industrialized countries which, although not perhaps exciting for one's own exports, can be expected to set up competitive production for export to the countries where one's own design is not being registered. If the list is too large, it may be necessary to prune it by eliminating, first, countries such as France, where protection is afforded under the copyright law anyway; second, countries such as West Germany, where a design registration is less valuable because copying must have taken place to win a design infringement action; third, countries such as the US, where only a close imitation constitutes an infringement of a design registration; and finally, countries such as Austria, Hungary and Italy, where the maximum life of a design registration is only three or four years.

If money is no object or the design is so important that a heavy expenditure is justified, then one should bear in mind the as yet under-developed countries. There is a growing tendency for large companies to set up production in countries which are not highly developed from an industrial point of view, the main attraction being low taxes and/or an abundant supply of relatively cheap labour. Examples of such countries are Ireland, Singapore, Malta, Portugal, Barbados, Mexico, Korea, Hong Kong and Taiwan. All of these countries either have statutory provisions of their own for design protection or the UK registration affords protection there automatically.

6.4 Prohibition on filing abroad

No UK resident may, without the Registrar's prior written permission, file a foreign design application (or cause it to be filed) in respect of a design relevant for defence purposes unless a UK application was filed at least six weeks earlier and no publication restriction is in force in the UK. The penalty for contravening this law is imprisonment or a fine or both.

6.5 Extension of UK registration abroad

The protection afforded by a UK design registration automatically extends to a considerable number of overseas territories, mostly

Countries to which a United Kingdom design registration extends automatically

Aden
Antigua
Barbados
Belize (formerly British Honduras)
Bermuda (local registration system also exists)
Botswana (formerly Bechuanaland)
British Solomon Islands
British Virgin Islands
†Cyprus
Dominica
Falkland Islands
Fiji
Gambia
Gibraltar
Gilbert Islands
Grenada
Guyana (local registration system also exists) (formerly British Guiana)
Hong Kong
Jamaica (local registration system also exists)
†Kenya
Lesotho (formerly Basutoland)
Malaya
†Malta (local registration system also exists)
†Mauritius
Montserrat
Sabah
Sarawak
St Christopher-Nevis and Anguilla
St Helena
St Lucia (local registration system also exists)
St Vincent
Seychelles
Sierra Leone
Singapore
Somali Republic (as applicable to the former British Somaliland)
Swaziland
†Tanzania
Tuvalu (formerly Ellice Islands)
†Uganda

† Signatory to the International Convention.

Fig. 6.2   List of countries to which a UK design registration
extends automatically　.

colonies or former colonies, as though an independent registration
had been obtained there. This is not by reason of any provisions in
the UK law but because of enactments in the respective countries,
many of which are uninteresting to most British manufacturers but

a few of which, such as Hong Kong, are extremely commercially important. Some years ago, the author researched all the relevant government ordinances and compiled a list of the countries in question. This list is being kept up to date by the Industrial Property Department of the Department of Trade and Industry, who will provide the latest information. It is reproduced in Fig. 6.2. In most cases, it is provided that the UK registration is without effect in those territories where the design was already published or in use before the UK filing date.

Some people are under the misapprehension that in countries to which the UK design extends automatically it is nevertheless necessary to publish a press notice giving details of the UK registration and, especially, the drawings or photographs of the article bearing the design. The publication of these particulars makes not an iota of difference to the legal effectiveness of the UK registration abroad. What it does do is to serve as a warning to potential infringers and possibly enhance the proprietor's prestige and it might also, but this is problematic, make it more difficult for an actual infringer to escape the payment of damages in an infringement suit when pleading that he was an innocent infringer, the public notice then being cited as a counter argument to the plea of innocence.

6.6 International design registration

By agreement between certain countries, the number of which is far too small to justify the description 'international', a single design registration is obtainable, which is effective in all the countries that have adhered to the agreement. The principal participating countries (there are several small States which are also members) are Egypt, France, Federal Republic of Germany, German Democratic Republic, Indonesia, Spain, Switzerland and South Vietnam.

An application for an International registration is deposited with the International Bureau in Geneva, can claim priority from a foreign application if it is filed within six months, and must include representations or specimens, identify the articles to which the design is to be applied and name those of the participating countries to which the registration is to extend. The applicant, and anyone to whom he might later wish to assign the registration, must be a subject of one of the participating countries or a company organized under the laws of a participating country or someone domiciled or having a business in a participating country. In the country of origin (except in the case of Switzerland), the International registration must be supplemented by a local registration. The duration of the International registration is five years, renewable for a further period of ten years.

UK citizens and companies do not normally qualify for International design protection because the UK is not a participating country; but there is nothing to prevent, say, a British company from assigning the design to an associated company in a country that is a signatory to the agreement. The territory of the assignment from the British company could, if so desired, be restricted to certain of the countries who are signatories. The associated company can then avail itself of the International registration procedure. There are two points to watch: first, permission for an assignment may have to be obtained from the UK Registrar of Designs if no corresponding British design had been filed or if it was filed less than six weeks earlier and, second, the International registration can never become the property of the UK company.

7. *Artistic copyright and design copyright*

7.1 Introduction to copyright law

The preceding chapters of this book have been concerned with the law and procedure affecting the protection of industrial designs by the registration system as laid down in the Registered Designs Act and Rules. It has been indicated in section 1.12 that considerable overlap exists between the Designs Act and the Copyright Acts but, although the overlap has existed since 1968, it is only very recently that the significance of this overlap has begun to be appreciated in industry, and not fully appreciated at that. The law regulating artistic copyright is the Copyright Act 1956, which is intricate and has been modified by amending legislation which took effect in October 1968 and is known as the Design Copyright Act 1968. As a result of this latter Act, there was at first a wide conflict of opinion amongst members of the legal profession about the precise extent to which industrial designs are the subject of artistic copyright. Sweeping statements were made by some who believed that the copyright law was now the answer to the businessman's prayers and rendered design registrations superfluous and others who maintained that this was nonsense, that copyright hardly subsisted in industrial designs at all. Neither view proved to be correct but it is small wonder that the businessman remains confused. Manufacturers and importers whose concern it is to obtain a measure of protection for their products without becoming involved in legal disputes on technicalities have rightly chosen the safe course of relying on the registration procedure under the Designs Act and, for reasons that will become clear, they should continue to do so. However, there will always be cases where a design is unregistrable or the opportunity to obtain a design registration has been missed and recourse is attempted to the copyright law, which does not require a work to be registered, or, conversely, where it may have been decided to copy a seemingly unprotected (unregistered or invalidly registered) design, only to find that the author is trying to enforce his copyright. It is therefore deemed to be essential to the scope and purpose of this book to set out the principles of artistic copyright and its practical effect on industrial design protection.

7.2   Artistic copyright in plans

Until a Court of Appeal judgment was delivered in the classic case of *Dorling v. Honnor Marine* (next section), the law was generally believed to be that a monopoly in the form of Letters Patent or a design registration is granted to the deviser of an invention or to the author of an industrial design in return for having enriched the art by disclosing particulars of his invention or design to the public in a formal application and in such a way that anyone might later be free to copy, that is to say copy the invention or design after the statutory period of the monopoly has expired or even earlier if the patent or registration has been allowed to lapse prematurely or has been revoked. This tenet was summarized by Lord Justice Fletcher Moulton in a 1906 decision and was certainly correct at the time:

> . . . in all these cases the basis of the legislation is that persons who do anything original in the way of the designing or making of an invention are allowed a monopoly for a time, but only on terms that they so publish to the public their original work that at the end of the time the public may have the full benefit of it. That applies as well to Designs as it does to Letters Patent.

If the inventor or author has not availed himself of the registration procedure then, so it used to be said, he has forfeited every right to protection. Consequently, it was common practice for a manufacturer to instruct a search amongst granted patents and design registrations to see whether he would be safe to copy a competitor's product; if there was no patent or registration, or where there had been one but it was no longer in force, he felt free to copy even the minutest details. He would have been wrong to continue with this practice after the Copyright Act 1956 came into force because there is the previously discussed exception in the Designs Act, which states that designs for certain articles primarily of a literary or artistic nature are excluded from registration; such articles are instead eligible for copyright protection (which is granted automatically, i.e., without a registration procedure) and must therefore be respected for the very many years that copyright remains in force. Also, it was suspected but, judging from the surprise caused by the Dorling case, never taken quite seriously that copyright subsists automatically in drawings and plans that are commonly prepared before going into production. It was no doubt because of this apparent disbelief that manufacturers were invariably advised: if there is no current patent or design registration, go ahead and copy.

The fact is that, even if the article in question was not one disqualified from registration by reason of being primarily of a literary or artistic nature, but had a shape dictated solely by its function or was strictly hand-made or was otherwise ineligible for design registration, an original drawing might be in existence of which the copyright could nonetheless be infringed. Artistic copyright subsists in original production drawings (until 50 years after the author's death) and even under the Copyright Act of 1911 (which excluded protection for designs intended to be applied industrially) it was established that this copyright is infringed when the two-dimensional drawing is copied in three dimensions. One relevant decided case has already been referred to in section 2.17; it was pronounced in 1916 that the copyright in drawings of type faces would be infringed by the matrices for casting the type. Further, in 1949 it was stated in the House of Lords, in what is known as the 'Popeye' case, '. . . an industrial object, whether in two or three dimensions, may well be an infringement of the artistic copyright in the preliminary drawings or prints made by the author in the design registered . . . .' Indeed, it was held that the artistic copyright in cartoons was infringed by dolls and brooches. At that time, the author's intention when creating the artistic work was still decisive. If there was initially no intention of making industrial products corresponding to the artistic work, these later products were covered by the copyright protection.

In 1952 there was presented to Parliament a report from the Copyright Committee (Cmnd 8662) which was charged with considering what changes, if any, should be made to the copyright law. The Committee commented in relation to industrial designs:

It does seem to us to be inequitable that, in certain circumstances dependent upon the original intention of the artist, industrial designs (such as 'Popeye' dolls and brooches) can have automatic protection for 50 years or more under the Copyright Act while most industrial designs are only protected for a maximum of 15 years and then only if they are registered under the Designs Act.

This criticism was acted upon in 1956 (see section 7.4).

7.3 The famous case of *Dorling v. Honnor Marine*

The defendant made and sold kits of parts for a build-it-yourself sailing dinghy, as well as photographs of the parts and of the completed dinghy, in alleged contravention of the copyright in plans owned by the designer. There was no design registration for the dinghy or its parts and therefore the trial judge had ruled that the plaintiff (a) had forfeited all the rights he could have acquired by registration, including the exclusive right to manufacture his design of dinghy for sale and to make anything (such as a kit of parts or photographs) for enabling the dinghy to be made, and (b) had, by reason of certain provisions in the Copyright Act, lost his artistic copyright in the plans.

The Court of Appeal held otherwise, one of the appeal judges applying the following reasoning. The plans for the dinghy could never have been registered because plans are specifically excluded from registration under the Registered Designs Act. The plaintiff therefore enjoyed copyright in the plans (irrespective of the artistic merit of that which was shown in the plans). The Designs Act would have given the plaintiff—had he registered his design of the dinghy as a whole—the right to prevent others from making for sale an article which looked like the completed dinghy, but not a monopoly for making parts of an article shown in detail in the unregistrable plans. Nor did the kit of parts (as distinct from, say, a mould or die) constitute things made for enabling the dinghy to be made. The plaintiff could therefore not have obtained protection for the parts under the Designs Act and was eligible for protection under the Copyright Act. The Court of Appeal found that the copyright in the plaintiff's plans had been infringed by the defendant's kit of parts in so far that the kit was clearly a three-dimensional copy of the plans (a fact that could be established without needing expertise in reading the plans) and also infringed by the defendant's photographs which were a two-dimensional copy of a three-dimensional copy of the protected two-dimensional plans.

The soundness and scope of application of this judgment was disputed in several quarters, the argument being that industry would become paralysed; but it remains the law and industry has not become paralysed. The case is of great importance because it at least confirms that one cannot slavishly copy a competitor's product, certainly not as far as strictly functional unregistrable features and parts of articles are concerned, without running the risk of infringing the copyright that automatically exists, irrespective of artistic merit, in original plans of the product.

7.4 Overlap between copyright and design laws

In 1968 the Copyright Act 1956 was amended by the Design Copyright Act to make it possible for some (not all!) industrial designs to enjoy copyright protection notwithstanding their registrability under the Designs Act. Since opinions differ as to exactly which designs are affected and little has been published on the subject to explain to the layman the considerations that are involved, it is deemed necessary to discuss the matter at greater length here than one would otherwise wish to do in a book that is to be kept simple.

Before the Copyright Act 1911 (which is still applicable to artistic works made before 1 June 1957), there was practically no overlap between the copyright and design laws. The 1911 Act then introduced a prohibition on the unauthorized copying of two-dimensional works by three-dimensional reproductions but made provision for excluding from artistic copyright protection those designs which were used or 'intended to be used' as models or patterns to be multiplied by any industrial process. The previously mentioned Copyright Committee, after considering the changes that ought to be made to the 1911 Act, recommended that copyright should continue to subsist in an original drawing but irrespective of whether it was the author's intention at the time he created the work to use it as, or apply it to, an industrial design.

The 1956 Act adopted this recommendation. On the one hand, the same degree of overlap was maintained as in the 1911 Act but, on the other hand, double protection for industrial designs was avoided in terms so that the intention of the copyright author at the time of making the work would no longer be material. In simplified language, here is what the 1956 Act said before it was amended in 1968; the summary is included because it may well be decided by Parliament to revert to this former law.

(a) Where a design corresponding to an artistic work has been registered, it shall not be an infringement of copyright to do anything that falls within the scope of the Designs Act, even after the registration has expired.

(b) Where a design corresponding to an artistic work has not been registered and, with the copyright owner's permission, articles have already been marketed to which the design has been applied industrially (applied to more than 50 articles which are not part of a set or applied to goods made in lengths or pieces), it shall not be an infringement of copyright to do anything that would have fallen within the scope of the Designs Act if a corresponding design had been registered.

Accordingly, the 1956 Act again prescribed that you must look to the Registered Designs Act if you want protection for an artistic work used for or applied to an industrial design. If protection was not available by registration then you could resort to the Copyright Act, namely for articles mainly of a literary or artistic character and for industrial designs made from drawings of parts of articles or purely functional articles.

These provisions have now been cancelled by the Design Copyright Act 1968—a change that was not recommended by the 1962 Departmental Committee Report on Industrial Designs. What the 1968 Act has done is to provide automatic protection (amounting to outright double protection if the design is also registered) for any industrial design which corresponds to an artistic work.

7.5 Artistic copyright in the design itself

It will now be evident that the design registration procedure and the previously described artistic copyright in original plans or drawings for unregistrable designs do not exhaust the forms of protection available to industrial designs. Artistic copyright not only continues to subsist automatically in all those designs which are barred from registration under the Designs Act—for example, designs applied to medals, stamps, maps and dress-making patterns—but, for the first time, automatic copyright protection in an industrial design corresponding to an artistic work can exist side by side with protection by way of design registration. This concept is still so fundamentally new in the affected trade circles that it is worthwhile to give the reader a paraphrased rendering of the relevant part of the current copyright law.

Where copyright subsists in an artistic work and a corresponding design is, with the authority of the copyright owner, applied industrially to articles marketed anywhere in the world, then after 15 years from the date of first marketing the articles it shall not be an infringement of copyright in the artistic work to do anything that would, if the corresponding design had been registered, have fallen within the scope of the Designs Act for that design and for all associated designs and articles. The expression 'all associated designs and articles' means every possible modified design that could have been registered under the provisions described in section 2.34 and all the articles to which the design, or any modified design, is capable of being applied. If the design in question was incapable of registration by reason of the article being excluded from registration (section 2.6 *et seq.*), these provisions do not apply, so copyright in the artistic work continues to subsist until 50 years from the author's death.

As is so often the case, the wording of the Copyright Act is in negative terms. While the amended Act does not state positively that copyright protection is afforded to industrially applied designs, the implication is certainly there and the courts have so held.

The 1968 amending Act came into operation on 25 October 1968 and is not retroactive, but copying has been unlawful since that date. It has already been mentioned that the period of automatic copyright protection for designs is 15 years from first marketing—to be more precise, 15 years beginning with the date on which articles to which the design has been applied were first sold, let for hire or offered for sale or hire anywhere in the world. Note that the copyright in the actual artistic work to which the design corresponds (for example an original drawing) continues in force for the full 50 years plus.

7.6 The law of artistic copyright

By reason of the amending Act in 1968, the copyright law nowadays has such a far reaching effect on the protection of industrial designs that it is appropriate at this stage to consider some fundamental aspects—but only in so far as they are applicable to artistic works in relation to designs.

Basically, and as the name implies, copyright is the right to copy and this right is infringed by an unauthorized copy. Artistic copyright is the exclusive right to do, and authorize others to do, certain acts in relation to a work, or a substantial part of that work, in the UK or in any of the many 'included' countries to which the Act is applied. These 'included' countries are stipulated by Order in Council and in fact comprise all member countries of the Berne Copyright Union, all parties to the Universal Copyright Convention and most British territories and colonies—in short, all the important industrial countries in the world except the People's Republic of China. The 'certain acts' just referred to are, as far as artistic works are concerned, publishing the work, reproducing the work, or a substantial part of the work, in any material form and including the work in a television broadcast. A reproduction in any material form includes a two-dimensional reproduction of a three-dimensional work and a three-dimensional reproduction—if recognized as such by a non-expert—of a two-dimensional work. It should be observed that copyright does not reside in an idea but in the work embodying the idea. The idea is not protected.

7.7   Infringing acts

For practical purposes, we can concentrate on the case where the copyright in an industrial design is infringed by someone who, without permission from the copyright owner or his licensee, copies at least a substantial part of the design or instructs another person to do so. The act of copying need not be deliberate to constitute an infringement. The question whether a substantial part of the copyright work has been taken by an infringer depends more on the quality than the quantity of what has been copied. Artistic copyright is also infringed by an importer of the infringing article to the UK (or to one of the included countries) but only if the importer knew that the making of the article constitutes copyright infringement or would have constituted copyright infringement if the article had been made in the country of importation. However, the importation must have been other than for private and domestic use.

Copyright is further infringed by someone who—and again this applies to the UK or any included country—sells, lets for hire, offers for sale or exhibits or distributes for trade purposes any article the making of which he knew to be a copyright infringement. It is not an infringement to deal with a work by way of research or private study or for the purpose of criticism and review (if accompanied by a sufficient acknowledgment), nor to reproduce a work by sketches or photography if it is permanently situated in a public place, nor to reproduce a work for the purpose of judicial proceedings.

If infringement has been found by the court, the plaintiff (namely, the copyright owner or his exclusive licensee) may obtain relief by way of an injunction and damages. The damages recoverable in copyright actions can, under certain circumstances, go far beyond those outlined in section 5.30.

7.8 Conditions for copyright to subsist

For copyright to subsist in an artistic work it must be original. Also, its first publication must have taken place in the UK or an included country or the author must have been a 'qualified' person at the time of first publication or, if he died before publication, immediately before his death. As far as artistic copyright is concerned, a qualified person is one who is a British subject or British protected person, or a citizen of the Republic of Ireland, or someone who is domiciled or resident in the UK or in an included country (see section 7.6).

7.9 Copyright owner

Artistic copyright is owned by the author of the work, unless the work was made in the course of the author's employment under a service or apprenticeship contract or there was some agreement to the contrary. If the work is commissioned, an assignment of the copyright to the beneficial owner is required in writing. A specific assignment must also be drawn up for a work made by a director, who is not regarded as an employee unless his contract mentions that his duties include the designing of products. For a photograph, incidentally, the author is defined as the person who owned the photographic material at the time the photograph was taken. The right to publish and reproduce the work in one or several forms can be assigned or licensed by the author or the beneficial owner in much the same way as other property.

There can be more than one author of a single work. Joint authorship is involved if the work is produced by the collaboration of two or more persons, the contribution by each author being inseparable from that of the co-author(s). Someone who suggests the idea for the work without contributing anything else is not a co-author; nor is a person who revises a work by making minor additions or alterations. Again, there is no joint authorship if the

contribution to a collective work by each author is clearly disting-
uishable and divisible from that of the other(s).

It is emphasized that an artistic work belongs to the employer
only if the work was made in the course of employment under a
contract of service. In one copyright infringement action, it was
agreed that the copyright in three of the drawings made by the
managing director was being held in trust for his company and
would have to be assigned to the company on demand. Since there
had been no actual assignment before the action was brought and,
since the managing director was not personally a party to the
action, his three drawings were disregarded.

7.10 Duration

Copyright in an artistic work subsists until 50 years from the end of
the calendar year in which the author died. There are some special
cases with which we need not concern ourselves here and, of
course, the previously discussed important exception of 15 years in
the case of works where a corresponding registrable design has
been industrially applied to articles.

7.11 Originality

A prerequisite for copyright protection is that the artistic work be
original in the sense of being the author's own work that required
some measure of judgment or skill and labour, as distinct from the
meaning of the word in the registered designs law. Originality in
thought or research is not required because copyright subsists in
the work and not in the idea that inspired the work. It is therefore
the skill and/or effort in applying a concept—in bringing the work
into existence—that needs to be original. There is no particular
required standard of novelty (or artistic merit); as long as the
author exerted independent skill and labour in executing the work,
the condition of originality is satisfied no matter how closely the
result might resemble an earlier work. Even if the author enlisted
the aid of existing works to execute his own, it is possible for his
work to be protected by copyright. For example, he might need to
exercise skill and labour to make a compilation, say a trade
catalogue from existing material, or evolve a three-dimensional
object from a drawing, or collect and select existing information
and arrange the results in tabular form, and so on. It should be
noted that copyright may under certain circumstances be enjoyed

by original works that were made in contravention of someone else's rights. Thus, if a reader were to translate this book, he would be infringing the copyright owned either by the author or his publisher, depending upon the arrangement made between them, but this would not entitle another person to copy the infringing but original translation in which copyright also subsists.

7.12 Artistic work

The Copyright Act defines an artistic work as any painting, sculpture (including a cast or model made for purposes of sculpture), drawing (including a diagram, map, chart or plan), engraving (including an etching, lithograph, woodcut or print) and photograph (including a product of any process akin to photography)—all irrespective of artistic quality. An artistic work is also any work of architecture or any work of artistic craftsmanship (but not irrespective of artistic quality!). Artistic craftsmanship is discussed in a later section.

7.13 Summary of artistic copyright

Artistic copyright subsists in published and unpublished original works as soon as they are made and there is no depositing or registration procedure in the UK. The author is not necessarily the beneficial owner of the work. For example, if he originated the work while being employed, the employer may be the rightful owner under the law of master and servant. Copyright used to be of interest to industry only as far as advertisements, brochures, instruction leaflets, catalogues and illustrated packagings and unregistrable designs are concerned but, under the amended Copyright Act, designs corresponding to artistic works are also protected by copyright. The copyright in plans can be infringed directly by a locally made or imported three-dimensional product copied from the plans but only if a layman can recognize the infringing product as being a replica of the two-dimensional plans. Alternatively, it is more likely that an infringer, whether he be resident here or abroad, will have copied the copyright owner's product without having had sight of the protected drawings; a copy of the copyright owner's product will then constitute indirect infringement of the drawings from which the legitimate product was made—again, provided that the infringing product is clearly recognizable from the drawings by an unskilled person. If, therefore, the original drawings are intricate technical representations, care should be taken to include at least one clear assembly or pictorial view of the finished product. Most important, all original plans and sketches should be carefully preserved and a record kept of the author's identity.

Designs are sometimes also developed by fashioning or constructing a prototype or model which can be termed an artistic work and from which the articles to be sold are then made, possibly by making a cast or mould. Unauthorized copies may infringe the copyright in such a prototype or original model, which should be carefully preserved for presenting in evidence when the need arises. It may not help much to keep a production sample as evidence because the production sample is unlikely to have been made by the author of the artistic work and would therefore not be his original work; nor would a drawing made from the prototype. For the same reason, an original drawing or sketch is preferred to a blueprint of it, although the one-time existence of an original might be conceded if the blueprint is produced.

The court recognizes that in most cases it will be impossible for the plaintiff to establish copying beyond all doubt, even if there has been an order for discovery. A *prima facie* case can therefore be made out by showing that the works are too similar to permit one to assume that the allegedly infringing work was conceived independently. The case is strengthened if peculiarities, such as mistakes, are reproduced in the defendant's work and evidence is available that the plaintiff's work, or a reproduction of it, was accessible to the defendant (such as through an employee who left to join the defendant). The onus of proof will then shift to the defendant who must show that he did not copy, or rather show how his work came into being independently. Note that the court will have to be satisfied that the plaintiff's and defendant's designs were not both copied from an even earlier work.

Finally, it should be emphasized that, by reason of the very many included countries to which the 1956 Act is applied as far as the country of origin or first publication of the work is concerned, and having regard to the fact that imports to the UK or to one of the included countries also constitute infringements, there is hardly any territorial limit for artistic copyright protection under the law of the UK. Of course, an importer (or anyone else who deals in, as distinct from makes, offending products by way of trade) is guilty of an offence only if he knew that his articles infringed the copyright law, but it is an easy matter for the copyright owner to draw an offender's attention to the position and thereafter the infringer continues the offending activities at the risk of facing a court action. Innocence is not a defence for the person who made the infringing work. A foreign copyright owner (provided the author was a 'qualified person' at the time of first publication or the artistic work was first published in one of the included countries) can bring an action in the British courts against a UK infringer regardless of whether the imitations were made in the UK. Conversely, if a British copyright owner carefully preserves his original drawings of a product and preferably also marks them, and the products, with the internationally recognized designation of a capital letter C in a circle followed by his name and the year of first publication, he may find it possible to found an action against imitators in a foreign country but this will depend on the laws of the country in question.

7.14   Why copyright in a design?

One wonders why it should have been necessary to afford copyright protection for a design which corresponds to an artistic work and which has been industrially applied to an article. The copyright law was already applicable to unregistrable artistic designs and to the original drawings from which articles with unregistrable designs were made, while the design law made adequate provision for giving a monopoly in industrial designs for a maximum period of 15 years. These forms of protection remain entirely unaffected by the 1968 Copyright Act. Why, then, also provide for artistic copyright for roughly 15 years in works from which certain industrial designs are derived? The legislators of this country are so overworked that one would expect some pressing need for the 1968 Act. In fact, the bill was introduced to Parliament by a member who sought to help jewellers and toy makers in her constituency to obtain protection against copying by oriental countries. No one seemed to appreciate that the existing law already afforded fast, adequate and cheap protection by the registration system and automatic free copyright protection for unregistrable designs.

It should not be imagined that the effect of the 1968 Copyright Act has been to eliminate the injustice, shown up again by the Dorling case, of affording over 50 years of protection to the drawings of designs applied to unregistrable articles. This is not what has been achieved. True, anything that would have been an infringement under the Designs Act ceases to be an infringement under the Copyright Act 15 years from first marketing; but it is stipulated that articles excluded under the Designs Act remain unaffected. Consequently, drawings of these excluded articles continue to be protected (and continue to be infringed by three-dimensional reproductions) until 50 years from the author's death. We therefore now have the extraordinary anomaly of 15 years of copyright protection being afforded to the drawings of registrable industrial designs (as far as reproduction in three-dimensional form is concerned) and 50 years plus to the drawings of unregistrable industrial designs—a truly amazing situation if one considers that the work and skill involved in creating both types of drawings might be the same and that the artistic merit of what is actually shown in the drawings is immaterial anyway.

7.15 Corresponding design

According to the Copyright Act, 'corresponding design' in relation to an artistic work means a design which, when applied to an article, results in a reproduction of that work or a substantial part of the work. This is one of the few definitions in the Act that seems to be self-explanatory. The definition of 'artistic work' has already been given.

7.16 Not all designs are affected

Having established that, for some inexplicable reason, 'corresponding designs' are now given automatic copyright protection, it remains to be investigated just which designs fall into this category. Some experts were convinced that most designs would be eligible for copyright protection and that the registration system was now redundant. It is difficult to see how this conclusion can be justified. It appears to have been overlooked entirely by those who have ventured to give an opinion on the subject that the opening words of the relevant section of the Copyright Act are: 'Where copyright subsists in an artistic work and a corresponding design is applied industrially . . .' Before everything else, therefore, copyright must subsist in an artistic work. Only after the existence of an artistic work has been established and only if it can be shown that copyright still subsists in the artistic work can one probe into the question of whether a corresponding design which has been applied to articles is protected by the copyright in the artistic work. Now, by reason of the definition in the Copyright Act, a drawing is undoubtedly an artistic work and in many cases, but by no means all cases, industrial designs are preceded by original drawings. Perhaps it was with drawings in mind that a High Court judge in a motion for an interlocutory injunction concerning the copying of drawings of light fittings stated, in passing:

> Whereas, therefore, under the unamended Copyright Act the position was that no copyright protection for an industrial design was given unless it was registered in accordance with the Registered Designs Act 1949, the position now is that copyright protection under the amended Copyright Act arises immediately and is given to industrial designs which are also artistic works for 15 years as if they had been registered under the Registered Designs Act. There is now, therefore, no need to register also under the Registered Designs Act, but it is not prevented.

This remark is believed to be an oversimplification of the situation. Copyright protection arises automatically, but not 'immediately'. Even if there is an artistic work and a corresponding design is industrially applied to articles, there will be no protection for the design before the articles are marketed. Also, it is already becoming apparent that there will often be occasions where a design registration is of benefit and perhaps even the only enforcible protection. What happens in the doubtlessly frequent cases where the drawing cannot be understood by a layman or the date of the drawing or its authorship or the devolution in title cannot be established or perhaps even the original drawing has not been kept? And what about the very many designs that are developed without preliminary drawings? The implication that a design registration is now a rather superfluous optional procedure is submitted to be wrong.

7.17 Artistic craftsmanship

The definition of artistic work includes any work of artistic craftsmanship, so a design corresponding to such a work is now likewise protected automatically for 15 years under the 1968 Copyright Act but 'artistic craftsmanship' is nowhere defined. The term was once discussed in relation to 'originality' in a case which was tried under the 1911 Copyright Act and concerned a frock made by craftswomen working from a designer's sketch. The judge commented as follows:

> It is said that, having regard to the beauty of this frock when completed, it is not only a work of craftsmanship but a work of artistic craftsmanship. For the moment, though I am not satisfied that that is correct, I will assume that it is. But where did the artistic element which has become connected with this work originate? It certainly did not originate in the work-people. All they did was by purely mechanical processes to produce the article. They are craftswomen, but they were not artistic craftswomen; they borrowed the artistic qualities of the article from the inspiration of Mrs Burke in her sketch, and accordingly, although I can well understand that it might be said that the frock was an original work of craftsmanship, the craftsmanship being original, it is not, in my view, an original work of artistic craftsmanship, because the artistic element did not originate in those who made the work. It is not original in so far as it is artistic; in so far as it is not artistic it is not protected by the Act. On that ground I cannot hold that the frock 'MLB 2' is an original work of artistic craftsmanship and I must, therefore, hold that the plaintiff company has not copyright in the frock 'MLB 2'. I can conceive it possible that Mrs Burke might design a frock and make it all herself, and if she did that I can well understand she might be the author of an original work of artistic craftsmanship, but that is not what has happened in this case. I do not want it to be assumed that, even so, I should feel able to hold that a lady who designed a frock and made it all herself was necessarily entitled to copyright. The point is not one which it is necessary for me to decide.

One wonders whether this comment was not too harsh. The judge was convinced that the work-people did not originate artistic craftsmanship and it will be noted that the question of whether a frock can ever be an original work of artistic craftsmanship was left undecided. It does not seem to have been considered that the very act of adapting a sketch for industrial purposes—working up the design by converting the sketch to a three-dimensional product—might require not only original work but also artistic skill.

With the advent of the 1968 Design Copyright Act, it was inevitable that there should soon be more case law to resolve conflicting opinions in the legal profession as to when an industrial design does or does not correspond to an original work of artistic craftsmanship. Almost the first case to come to trial in this respect went as far as the House of Lords. It concerned the alleged copyright infringement of certain chairs and settees produced from a prototype made by three authors working jointly, with the major contribution made by one of their group. Referring to the case of the frocks, and then pronouncing on the case in hand, the trial judge said:

> It seems to me that the case of Burke is quite a different one from the present case where, as I have found, there was quite clearly collaboration between Mr Hensher, Mr Sutton and Mr Batchelor, and where they all took part in the conception, embodiment and completion of the finished article. I do not therefore think that the Burke case is an authority which governs the present.
>
> My conclusion on this part of the case is therefore that these chairs and settees are works of artistic craftsmanship in that they have, whether one admires them or not, distinctive characteristics of shape, form and finish, which were conceived and executed by Mr Hensher and those working with him so as to result in articles which are much more than purely utilitarian. They exhibit in my judgment distinctive features of design and skill in workmanship which the words of definition 'artistic craftsmanship' on their proper construction in their context connote . . .
>
> Now, although the matter is, of course, one of construction and is not one for the witness, I agree, as will be clear from what I have already said, that the proper construction of the phrase 'a work of artistic craftsmanship' in the section in question does denote a work which, while it is the subject of craftsmanship, that is to say made or designed by craftsmen, at the same time has individual characteristics which distinguish it from a mere utilitarian work of craftsmanship which has no distinctive features of design. The matter is not a particularly easy one to put into words, but if one compares an ordinary plain kitchen chair of no artistic merit with, for example, a chair produced in the factory of Mr Chippendale, one can readily appreciate that, while the latter will clearly be regarded as a work of artistic craftsmanship, the former may well not be, although it may be very well made and could properly be described as a work of craftsmanship.

In view of what I have said the plaintiffs are, I think, entitled to claim that in the Bronx chair and the developments of it they have made works of artistic craftsmanship which give them copyright in accordance with the section.

In this same infringement action it was, incidentally, held that certain drawings that were in existence proved to be inadequate to enable an ordinary member of the public to conclude that the allegedly infringing articles constituted reproductions.

Although the aforementioned decision did not actually say how one can recognize a work of artistic craftsmanship when one sees it, it certainly made sense and threw some further light on the subject. There was, for example, the suggestion that a kitchen chair is not a work of artistic craftsmanship because it is not distinguished from a utilitarian article by any artistic feature. The case then went to the Appeal Court where the judgment was reversed. The following excerpts show why the appeal judges thought that chairs and settees did not qualify as artistic works in the way the trial judge had thought.

It seems to us that the judge has in effect come to the conclusion that in the field of furniture all that is needed to qualify as a work of artistic craftsmanship is a sufficient originality of design to qualify as a design under the Designs Act. Is this right in law? We do not think so. It seems to give no sufficient effect to the word 'artistic' in the definition of the 1956 Act. The phrase is not 'a work of craftsmanship of original design'. We are conscious of the need to avoid a judicial assessment of artistic merits. But we do not think it is beyond the scope of a judge to come to a conclusion on what is meant by a work of artistic craftsmanship in principle. In our judgment, if it can be said of a work of craftsmanship that it is an object which would be expected to be acquired or retained rather for its functional utility than for any appeal to aesthetic taste, it is not within the scope of the phrase 'other works of artistic craftsmanship'. Mere originality in points of design aimed at appealing to the eye as commercial selling points will not in our judgment suffice. In our judgment, it is clear that upon that basis the plaintiffs' products cannot qualify as works of artistic craftsmanship. The plaintiffs' suites are perfectly ordinary pieces of furniture. People may buy one because it looks better as a suite to be sat in than other suites on view, but that is not enough, even if they also think it looks nice. And in any event we cannot think that any save a negligible unintelligent minority would dream of buying one without testing by sitting in it . . .

. . . in order to qualify as a work of artistic craftsmanship, there must at least be expected in an object or work that its utilitarian or functional appeal should not be the primary inducement to its acquisition or retention.

The Appeal Court's decision was finally confirmed by the House of Lords who, however, unanimously rejected its test as to what constitutes a work of artistic craftsmanship. It was stated that the artistic character of an article gives a person pleasure or satisfaction or uplift when contemplating it but that 'artistic' is a word that needs no interpretation, its ordinary meaning being well understood. Whether or not a particular article qualifies as a work of artistic craftsmanship depends on the evidence. Various opinions were expressed as to whose evidence might be taken. 'If any substantial section of the public genuinely admires and values a thing for its appearance and gets pleasure or satisfaction, whether emotional or intellectual, from looking at it, I would accept that it is artistic although many others may think it meaningless or common or vulgar,' said Lord Reid, while Lord Morris looked for a 'general consensus of opinion among those whose views command respect'. In this same connection Lord Simon expected the most convincing evidence to be obtainable from acknowledged artist-craftsmen or their teachers. Lord Kilbrandon expected the intention of the craftsman himself to be material to the court's decision.

It is of interest to record that the aforementioned Copyright Committee, when expressing the view that some copyright protection is required to cover works of art other than paintings, drawings and sculptures, said that they were concerned with the unregistrable works of craftsmen, not with industrially manufactured articles 'artistically meritorious as many of these are', which can be protected under the Registered Designs Act. Thus, the Committee seemed to recognize that there is artistic merit in many industrially manufactured articles.

In the experience of the author of this book, a large number of industrial designs come into being by way of a prototype constructed by the designer. Can such a prototype ever be regarded as a work of artistic craftsmanship? The answer must be an unqualified yes, but, from what has been said, it will be clear that each case must be decided on its own merits and is decided on the available evidence. There is no difficulty in understanding the meaning of 'craftsmanship'. A work of craftsmanship is the result of a craftsman's labours, a craftsman being someone who works with skill and dexterity as distinct from a machine operator who pushes buttons to start and stop operations or who exerts an inartistic pull on a handle. What to look for is whether any manual skill was required in executing the prototype. No doubt most prototypes of articles embodying an industrial design will require a certain amount of fashioning by hand and therefore qualify as works of craftsmanship. It is the artistic quality of the work of craftsmanship that will be in question every time and it is impossible to provide any guideline for resolving this question because personal tastes are involved. The judge in a court of law may look for the same kind of qualities as are possessed by recognized works of art such as classical paintings and sculptures. An engineer may obtain uplift from clean geometric or streamlined outlines while many a young artist-craftsman and his tutor receive pleasure from abstract configurations. Having regard to modern art and the contemporary tastes of people who are enraptured by pieces of bent metal constructed by a craftsman and mounted on a wall panel, it would have been thought that any craftsman who expends skill and judgment in conceiving and making an eye-appealing prototype for a commercial product can legitimately claim to have produced a work of artistic craftsmanship—be it ever so mundane as a piece of machinery or a household item. However, possibly because of the lack of corroborating evidence to this effect, the House of Lords judgment does not support this opinion.

From a commonsense point of view, it is inconceivable that the drawing of a kitchen chair should be artistic (irrespective of artistic merit) and enjoy copyright that can be infringed by a three-dimensional copy, but the very same chair made by a craftsman as a prototype without a preliminary drawing is devoid of artistic quality and free to be copied (unless it is the subject of a registered design). A draughtsman is surely no more artistic in putting pencil to paper to draw a commonplace chair than is a craftsman who uses tools and materials to make the same chair. It is not very likely that a more generous interpretation of 'artistic craftsmanship' will be applied by the courts in future, even if the right kind of evidence is produced, because the House of Lords is the highest court in the land and its judgment will be used as a precedent. It is more likely that the law will be changed by amending or new legislation.

7.18 Conclusion

By reason of the uncertainties described, it will be wise for design owners always to apply for protection under the Registered Designs Act, especially when the original work is a prototype. However, for a potential copier the safe course is to assume that at least during the first 15 years or so the design proprietor has a cause of action under the copyright law, and perhaps even longer. The 1968 Act has already had an effect on industry. The advice given to manufacturers who wish to copy their competitors' products is far more cautious than it used to be and both manufacturers and traders are beginning to follow the advice by developing their own products independently. Some makers have stopped copying products altogether in cases where they were once willing to risk infringement of the copyright in certain drawings but are now reluctant to run the greater risk of infringement under the 1968 Copyright Act. Others are seeking advice as to how they might make a closely resembling product without being guilty of copyright infringement. To them, one can only say 'do not copy'. Even the conscious avoidance of copying by having the copyright work in front of you and making deliberate departures from it could result in an infringing work; but conscious avoidance of copying is nevertheless safer than subconscious copying after having once seen the original and then put it out of view. For the potential plaintiff, the following practical suggestions are offered to make it easier to succeed in enforcing copyright.

What the author of the artistic work should do

A. Make his original work without reference to a prior work and preferably in the form of a drawing (which is an artistic work qualifying for copyright, whereas the eligibility of a model or prototype or the product itself might be disputed, especially if made by someone else).

B. Include in the drawing at least one pictorial view which can be understood by someone unskilled in reading technical drawings (because a three-dimensional copy is a reproduction of a drawing only if recognizable as such by a non-expert).

C. Mark the drawing (or model) with the date and place of execution, his name, address and nationality, and a capital letter C in a circle (to help in establishing at a later date that he was a qualified person and that copyright still subsists in his work, and to be of possible assistance in enforcing the copyright abroad).

What the artistic copyright owner should do

D. Preserve the original artistic work (which will be needed in evidence to compare with an alleged infringement).

E. Record how he came into possession of the artistic copyright and keep supporting documentary evidence such as an employment contract, apprenticeship contract, consultancy agreement, will or assignment (because the ownership, and hence the devolution in title if he was not the author, must be proven in an infringement action). Any assignment should preferably include a guarantee from the author that the entire work is his and was produced without reference to anyone else's products, either directly or indirectly.

F. Keep a record of when and to whom copies of the artistic work are supplied (as possible evidence showing that the infringer had access to the work).

What the individual design owner should do

G. Keep a note of where the artistic work is kept (so that it can be produced in an infringement action).

H. Record how he came into possession of the right to apply the corresponding design industrially to articles and keep supporting documentary evidence (so that he can show that he is entitled to bring an infringement action).

I. Record the date on which, the place where and to whom (if not at an exhibition) an article embodying the design was first offered for sale or hire (to enable the commencement of the 15 year term of copyright to be proved).

J. Keep notes of the manufacturing techniques and procedures and the amount of original artistic craftsmanship required of the workers who apply the design (so that, if there is no original drawing, he need not rely on his memory when giving evidence in support of the product being an original work of artistic craftsmanship).

K. Keep particulars of any design application that may have been filed but refused (because artistic works to which refused designs correspond are entitled to 50 plus instead of 15 years of protection).

L. Mark the product with a capital letter C in a circle followed by the name of the artistic copyright owner and the year of first publication (to permit the copyright to be enforced in some foreign country which has made, or might make, provision for protecting artistic copyright in industrial designs). At the very least, the products should be marked 'design copyright' to serve as a warning to potential imitators.

It is worth mentioning that the copyright law varies from country to country but probably nowhere is it as far reaching in its scope of protection as in the UK. If a copyright owner knows in advance that he will wish to place reliance on copyright in other countries, the respective foreign laws should be considered at an early stage. In the US, for example, it would be highly desirable to file an application for copyright registration because registration is compulsory there before copyright can be enforced and early registration will avoid subsequent difficulties with regard to producing copies of the original work and proving devolution of title.

Finally, there follows an imaginary agreement to indicate the kind of terms that might apply when licensing copyright.

THIS AGREEMENT is made on the . . . . day of . . . . .between GEORGE MYRANTS (hereinafter referred to as 'the Author'), a British subject of . . . ., of the one part and LEXIQUE LIMITED (hereinafter referred to as 'the Licensee'), a company organized and existing under the laws of the United Kingdom, of . . . ., of the other part;

WHEREAS the Author is the author of and sole owner of copyright subsisting in an artistic work (hereinafter referred to as 'the Work') in the form of a signed drawing dated 8 April 1972, a copy of which drawing is attached hereto,

AND WHEREAS the Licensee is desirous of taking a licence under the copyright subsisting in the Work;

NOW IT IS AGREED AS FOLLOWS
1. The Author hereby confers on the Licensee the exclusive right in the United Kingdom or elsewhere to apply industrially to any article any design corresponding to the Work and to do all other acts to which a copyright owner is entitled under the provisions of the Copyright Act 1956 as amended by the Design Copyright Act 1968, including the right to grant sub-licences for a term not exceeding the term of this Agreement.
2. The rights hereby conferred shall not be assignable by either party without the written consent of the other party.
3. The term of this Agreement shall be for a period of 15 years from the first sale or offer for sale of any said article to which any said corresponding design has been applied but the Agreement

may be determined prematurely on three months' written notice given by the Licensee to the Author at any time after three years from the date hereof, save that the Author may determine this Agreement forthwith at any time whatsoever if the Licensee is wound up or if the Licensee's business is transferred or sold or if the Licensee is more than three months in arrears in his payments as hereinafter specified.

4. The Licensee shall mark each said article or require each said article to be marked with the designation © followed by the Author's or any subsequent copyright proprietor's name and the year of first publication.

5. The Licensee shall pay the Author a royalty of 5 per cent of the trade price before V A T of each said article sold by or for the Licensee and any sub-licensee, save that the royalty payable under this Agreement shall be reduced to 0 per cent for said article on which a royalty is payable under any separate agreement concluded between the Author and the Licensee in respect of a registration under the Registered Designs Act or the equivalent law in foreign countries for any said corresponding design.

6. The Licensee shall render accounts to the Author at six-monthly intervals, commencing nine months from the date hereof, in respect of an accounting period terminating six months from the date hereof and every successive period of six months thereafter. All royalties due to the Author under this Agreement are payable within four months of termination of each accounting period and shall thereafter be considered to be in arrears if not paid. Every account shall show the number of articles sold during the respective accounting period and their trade price and shall identify those articles which are the subject of any such separate agreement as is referred to in paragraph 5 above.

7. The Author may have the Licensee's books, records and documents inspected by a Chartered Accountant, the cost of such inspection to be borne by the Licensee only if a discrepancy is found between the said books, records and documents and the accounts as rendered in accordance with paragraph 6 above.

8. This Agreement shall be construed and enforced under English law.

7.19 Reported cases

Reported copyright infringement actions, where it was pleaded that there was infringement of a design corresponding to an artistic

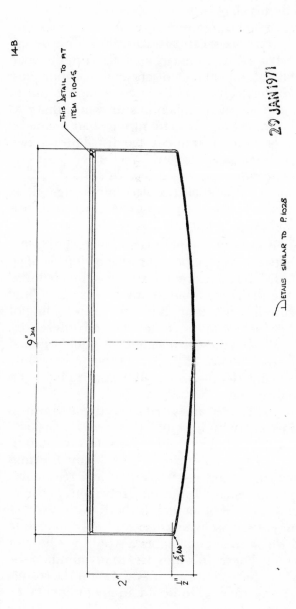

Fig. 7.1 Electric light fittings; drawing sued upon in a copyright action

work in the form of a drawing, include the following cases not previously described in this chapter.

(a) Imported electric light fittings (interim injunction to restrain infringement granted). This was a case of a basically simple design for a light fitting. In fact, it was its simplicity or, as the judge termed it, its modern clean line of appearance of attractive proportions, that made it a tremendous commercial success at home and in many countries abroad. One of the plaintiff's drawings that was sued upon is reproduced in Fig. 7.1. The fittings had created a sensation at the Hanover Trade Fair and a sole distributor agreement was signed with a German company which later went into production on its own account and was successfully sued in Germany. Another German company also copied the fittings; these were exported to the UK and it was the UK purchaser who was now being sued. Said the judge:

> If the defendants' fittings are compared with the plaintiffs' the great similarity between the shapes and proportions is obvious. The defendants' diffusers are flat, whereas the plaintiffs' are shown to be slightly domed, but, to my eye, this is of little materiality and certainly not enough to prevent a finding of infringement. There are, of course, other detailed differences, particularly internally, but these to my mind are equally immaterial, the overall resemblence of the fittings being very close and their shape being clearly and readily ascertainable on inspection of the drawings . . .
>
> It was argued by Mr Skone James that no sectional drawings could ever be infringed by a complete three-dimensional object constructed from those sections. This, to my mind, is going too far, and as I see it, is one of degree. Many drawings whether sectioned or not are so simple that any reasonably intelligent person can visualize what they represent in three-dimensional form. On the other hand, there are drawings, both sectioned and otherwise which are extremely difficult to understand and which many non-experts would get little or nothing out of at all. These drawings are, to my mind, in the first category and not the second and would, I think, be readily understood by a non-expert, who would, in my judgment, be entitled to look at the whole series of drawings, including the legends which say in general terms what the drawings are representing. That he would be entitled to look at the series is I think clear from the 'Popeye' case, where there was a very large number of drawings representing 'Popeye' in various attitudes

and forms, and it was not possible to say that the infringement was the same as any one drawing in particular. So here, in my judgment, an inspection of the drawings produces in the mind a clear impression of cylindrical and square fittings with clean side lines produced by the form of snap-on joints illustrated, the proportions and angles being also illustrated. This impression is embodied both in the plaintiffs' and defendants' fittings. For the reasons I have given, the plaintiffs have in my judgment made out a *prima facie* case of infringement of their copyright.

(b) Part of a shirt for clergy (action unsuccessful because a substantial part of the sketches had not been copied). The judge made the following comment, confirming the previous understanding of the term 'original' in a copyright sense:

> In his speech, Counsel for the defendants urged upon me that the evidence established that the Gleeson type of shirt was known in this country and the United States for years before 1959. This, again, is in essence really only a fringe matter, because, even if it were known, that could provide no defence if copying were established.

(c) Knitted fabrics (infringement found). This is an interesting case meriting more detailed consideration. The plaintiff's design director was in the habit of first making a sketch of a new design, and then preparing a drawing or graph from the sketch, the drawing or graph being known as a 'point pattern' which indicates the settings required for the knitting machine components so that the desired pattern is produced in the desired colours. In other words, the point pattern constitutes a set of instructions to the knitting machine operator. One of the defence witnesses admitted that the repeat fabric in question was prepared from point patterns worked out by the defendants themselves from a sample of unknown origin submitted by their customer. The witness mentioned that in this trade manufacturers have for many years been making repeats from samples produced by the customers— samples of which the origin would be unknown and difficult to establish—but that it was unheard of to consider whether copyright might be infringed by making the repeats. If, the witness said, a UK manufacturer is prevented from making knitted fabrics in this way because of copyright considerations, then the customer is bound to go to a manufacturer in, say, Germany where there is no restriction.

It was held that point patterns are drawings or diagrams (lines drawn on paper) and therefore artistic works, and that the material parts of these works had been taken. The judge remarked that fabric manufacturers will just have to come to terms with the position that original works are protected in the UK and indiscriminate copying in the absence of a patent or design registration is no longer permissible since the Design Copyright Act of 1968. The author of this book ventures to add that, although it may be a hardship for UK manufacturers to relinquish the trade in repeat patterns for fabrics to competitors in countries where there is no broad copyright protection commensurate with the law in the UK, the copyright law must be respected; it is, however, comforting to know that repeats made abroad will not be able to reach the UK market without the risk of a copyright infringement action. Consequently, UK customers for repeat patterns will be deterred from seeking out foreign manufacturers and there will be an incentive for having the repeat made by the copyright owner or his licensee.

(d) Front of an electric meter (infringement of sketch by one product proven; action unsuccessful on a second product). The following observations by the judge are worth quoting.

On the conscious avoidance of copying:

> The defendants say they did not have this Simpson meter in front of them when they made their re-design. Mr Dean also said that he did not have the Director 14 in front of him. This is perhaps surprising, since if one was genuinely endeavouring to avoid producing something in accordance with a previous meter of which complaint had been made one would expect that the draughtsman would say, 'I had better have the meter which is said has been copied in front of me so that I can make quite sure that my re-design avoids it.'

On the degree of ignorance required by a man to qualify as a non-expert for comparing alleged infringements with drawings:

> . . . the question to be decided seems to me to remain one of fact, and the court must do the best it can to put itself in the position of a non-expert, which fortunately it usually is, and must come to a conclusion on the matter having regard to the evidence and all the surrounding circumstances. In the present case, whilst the notional non-expert 'in relation to objects of that description' must presumably have no special knowledge of drawings of electric meters, I do not think it is right to

assume that he has no familiarity with engineering and similar drawings at all or that he is a particularly stupid or ill-informed person. If a normally intelligent person were given the S 528 Form 1 meter and Sketch No. 10 and asked whether it appeared to him that the former was a representation of the latter in three-dimensional form, I think he would be likely to answer that it was.

On the term 'original' in the copyright sense, which seems to come into dispute in almost every case:

There remains only the question whether the artistic work is 'original' within the meaning of section 3(2). There was some argument as to the meaning of the word 'original' and as to how far it was a necessary requirement that there should be more than the mere expenditure of time and labour by the author before a work could be said to be original.... The defendants put forward in this connection what may be called the 'squeeze' argument frequently met with in patent cases, when the defendant argues that if the claim of the patent is held to be broad enough to cover the alleged infringement it must be invalid as covering something else which is either old or obvious. Here they say the originality is so small when the plaintiffs' sketch is compared with the prior meter D.2 that if the plaintiffs' sketch is to be held original then its scope cannot be extended so far as to justify holding that the defendants' meters infringe. I do not consider that this is the proper way to approach copyright and its infringement, and if followed may produce very misleading results. Once it has been held that there is originality and that copyright subsists then, in my judgment, the proper question to be asked is, 'Has the defendant copied?', bearing in mind, of course, that at least a 'substantial part' of the work within the meaning of the Act must have been copied. This I have held to be the case here.

(e) Plastic divan leg (interim injunction to restrain infringement granted). Figure 7.2 shows the drawing, the copyright in which was alleged to be infringed and Fig. 7.3 illustrates a drawing made of the allegedly infringing product. Only one peculiar item of interest arose in this case; the judge described the position as follows:

The first point taken by the defendants here is that exhibit G.W.G.1 includes two drawings and therefore two artistic works and not one, and that each of those drawings must be

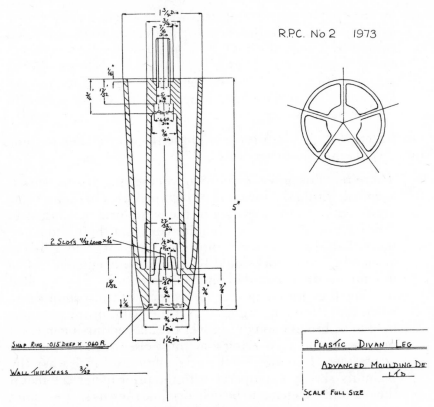

Fig. 7.2 Divan leg drawing sued upon in a copyright action

looked at separately. Their second point is that in looking at the drawings, and each of them, both the legend at the bottom 'Plastic divan leg' and 'Scale full size', and all the notations on the left-hand drawing showing such matters as sizes, diameters and thicknesses of the relative parts shown in the drawings must be ignored. They say this is so because artistic copyright cannot exist in an idea and the legend and figures convey ideas and are not artistic in themselves. I find this entirely unreal and take the view that where as here two sketches or drawings are included on a sheet and obviously relate to the same article they can both be looked at, both for the purpose of establishing the scope of the copyright and for considering purposes of infringement. Equally I think it is quite unreal when a section of an article is shown in the drawing to ignore the fact, as is clear from the wording, including the use of the word 'diameter', that it is a section of a circular article.

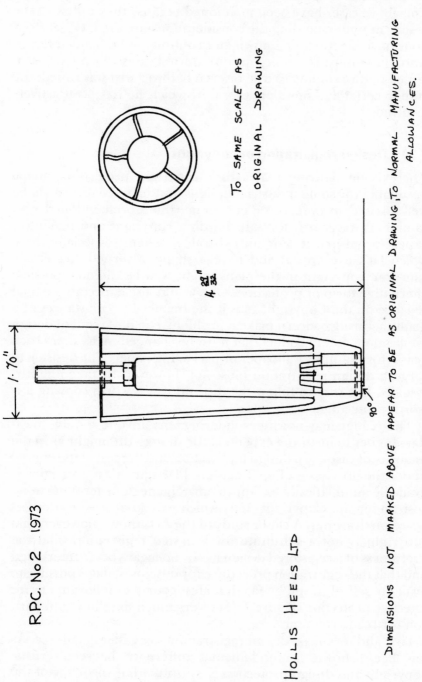

Fig. 7.3 Drawing of allegedly infringing divan leg

The above cases have been mentioned because they will assist the reader in understanding the considerations involved. Other decisions have been handed down and continue to be handed down. Also, there must be numerous unreported cases which have been settled before coming to trial or even before a writ was issued; the author certainly knows of several in which he has been actively involved.

7.20 Design registration or copyright?

There is no denying that artistic copyright protection can be invaluable for some industrial designs and manufacturers will be well advised to observe or encourage the aforementioned precautionary measures for safeguarding copyright and making it easier to enforce it. For unregistrable designs, especially those which lack eye appeal and have a shape governed entirely by function, copyright in the plans might well be the only possible alternative form of protection. One would also expect to see total reliance on the Copyright Acts if the financial circumstances of a manufacturing concern make it prohibitive to file frequent design applications for a product that must be changed many times each year—for example, wallpaper or packaging paper. The desision to forgo a design registration must not, however, be taken lightly. Usually, it is wise to follow the dictum: if it is worth copying it is worth protecting.

The reader may now be wondering why anyone should nowadays bother to incur the expense, little though this might be in the majority of cases, of a design registration and the cost of its renewal under the provisions of the Registered Designs Act if protection is available automatically for approximately the same term but at no cost under the Copyright Acts, which extend at least to designs based on drawings. A closer study of the Acts shows, however, that copyright is not a substitute for a design registration, that the usefulness of a registered design has by no means been superseded and that the registration procedure for designs is, if it is possible to avail oneself of it, still by far the safest course to follow to ensure effective protection. Figure 7.4 is a very much simplified comparison for ready reference.

First and foremost, design registrations are easier to enforce. As has been shown, a fundamental difference between artistic copyright and design protection is constituted by the scope of the protection that is afforded, which is broader in the case of the

	Copyright in *drawing* of unregistrable design	Copyright in unregistrable *artistic design*	Copyright in *design* industrially applied to articles	Registered industrial design
Eligibility for protection	Drawing must be original (in the copyright sense)	Design must be original (in the copyright sense), primarily of artistic or literary character or otherwise disqualified from registration	Design must correspond to an artistic work which is original (in the copyright sense)	Design must be new and original (in the sense of the Designs Act) and applied to a specified article)
Protection obtained	Automatically	Automatically	Automatically	By formal application
Maximum term	Life of author plus 50 years	Life of author plus 50 years	15 years from first marketing the articles anywhere	15 years from filing or priority date
Features protected	Illustrated features, regardless of artistic merit	Appearance of design	Appearance of design	Eye-appealing features, with reference to statement of novelty
Infringed by	Copying substantial part of drawing or making three-dimensional version of what is evident from drawing to a non-expert	Copying substantial part of articles embodying the design	Copying substantial part of articles embodying the design	Making the specified article, even by accident, if it looks substantially the same as the registered design

Fig. 7.4   Protection for designs: copyright compared with registration

monopoly granted by a design registration because the acts restrained by copyright are in effect limited to copying. An industrial designer is often concerned with simple articles, it being likely that another designer arrives at a similar design independently. Whereas in infringement proceedings under the Designs Act it is necessary to show only that the defendant's design is substantially the same as the registered design, under the Copyright Acts proof of copying is a prerequisite for a successful infringement action and even an identical version will be held not to infringe if the defendant can make it convincing that he produced his design independently.

The Design Copyright Act applies only to industrial designs corresponding to artistic works. Although it is clear that drawings are artistic works, very many designs indeed are not preceded by drawings and there remains more than just an element of doubt as to which works other than drawings qualify as works of artistic craftsmanship. It is therefore safer to rely on a design registration.

There is copyright infringement of plans by the design of a three-dimensional product only if a layman can recognize the identity between the products and the contents of the plans. Under the Designs Act it is bound to be easier to ascertain whether the alleged infringement is substantially the same as the registered design because pictorial representations accompany the registration and the task is not complicated by having to consider what a hypothetical non-expert can see in the drawings.

Copyright protection under the Design Copyright Act 1968 commences after the design has been applied to articles industrially, in fact from the date of first marketing the articles in any country, which is a date that may not always be easy to establish. A registered design could be effective sooner, namely from the date on which the registration certificate has issued. This is important, for example, in the case of an author who publishes but does not exploit his design immediately and who, if a competitor uses the same design industrially in the meantime, may find it difficult to stop the infringer because it is not clear that the copyright is enforcible until the author has also marketed articles. Even if the author can enforce the copyright in a drawing, he is faced with the task of proving that his drawing antedates the activities of the alleged copyright infringer and that a non-expert can clearly recognize the infringer's product as being a reproduction of the drawing.

Yet another point in favour of a design registration is the ease with which the ownership of the design can be established in infringement proceedings. In a copyright action, the original drawings or other work should still be available for production as evidence, devolution of title must be shown, and either the country of first publication of the artistic work must be proven or the author should be identifiable because he must, at the time of first publication, have been a person qualifying for copyright protection.

To be eligible for protection under the Design Copyright Act, the artistic work to which the design corresponds must have been executed by the author. Also, the design must have been 'applied industrially' but in some cases more than 50 articles embodying the design may not yet have been made by the time it is desired to start an infringement action. Under the Registered Designs Act, it is immaterial whether the proprietor of the protected design has already marketed articles embodying the design.

Despite its shortcomings, the Registered Designs Act is more definite and dependable than are the Copyright Acts, and it is supported and explained by more case law. A particularly uncertain aspect that arises with copyright is how much a work must resemble the original before it constitutes copyright infringement. With registered designs one can always use the yardstick that, in the absence of a specific statement of novelty, the overall appearance must be the same but in the case of copyright the author is likely to be more uncertain as to his rights. The Copyright Acts prevent others from reproducing the work in any material form or reproducing a substantial part of the work. An exact copy presents no difficulties but to determine whether a 'substantial part' has been copied involves guesswork.

Only a design application under the Registered Designs Act enables an author in this country to found a claim to priority under the International Convention for any foreign design application that is to be filed later. Also, a British design registration automatically extends to certain foreign territories and can therefore be enforced in these territories, whereas the Copyright Acts cannot.

A design registration is readily identified in licence or assignment documents by referring to its number but copyright in an artistic work, especially in a prototype, is more difficult to define. Also, agreements concerning copyright are not exempt from registration under the Restrictive Trade Practices Act 1956 and corresponding Common Market legislation and foreign legislation.

A design registration is granted in most cases only after an official novelty search has been conducted. This search is by no means exhaustive and certainly no guarantee of validity but it does have the effect that the registration often commands more respect in the commercial world than does automatic copyright which has passed no test at all.

A design registration receives an official number and many businessmen are of the opinion that to quote the number in trade literature and on the articles in question enhances prestige and has a commercial value in so far as competitors are deterred from bringing out similar products. It has also been said that it is a comfort to businessmen to receive a registration certificate as tangible evidence of the monopoly that has been granted whereas copyright protection is automatic and there is no reassuring piece of paper which one can show around as proof.

Finally, there is the argument that two forms of protection are better than only one.

For all these reasons, it is unwise to rely entirely on copyright protection, except in the case of purely functional features which are not registrable under the Designs Act and the designs of articles and parts of articles which are excluded from registration. The copyright law should rather be regarded as a useful complement for protection by way of a registered design. To consider the matter from another viewpoint, the wording as used in the Designs Act and the Copyright Acts is by no means the same and cases are always bound to arise where a design is an infringement under one Act but not the other, particularly if the evidence available to the plaintiff is inadequate to support an action under one of the Acts.

7.21   Stationers' Hall Registry

One of the difficulties with automatic copyright protection is that the proprietor needs to keep clear records and copies which he and his heirs or successors in business can trace and understand and the dates and authenticity of which are unlikely to be disputed. This difficulty is aggravated if devolution of title has to be proven for copyright that may have changed hands several times. Stationers' Hall Registry in London is a little-known organization which can be of assistance in this respect because for a fee it provides a facility for registering copies of books and fine arts and assignments of copyright therein. These registrations serve the purpose of providing an easily accessible record that may help to establish the existence and date of a work in subsequent infringement proceedings. No rights accrue from the registration and the Registry is not a government department. A copy of the work is deposited at the Registry. A certified copy of an entry in the register is issued when required. The entry is renewable every seven years. It is important to note that the books which are accepted for registration include published or unpublished maps, charts and all kinds of trade literature, while 'fine arts' includes drawings, designs, patterns, labels and photographs.

8. Other forms of design protection

8.1 Passing-off

Yet another, albeit rarely applicable, form of industrial design protection has already been mentioned in section 1.11. Under common law, it is an offence for a trader to pass off his goods as those of a competitor and thereby mislead the purchasing public and, in effect, steal the competitor's goodwill even though the act was not malicious or fraudulent. Such malpractice occurs most often when the competitor's trade mark is taken and/or the so called get-up is copied. However, the law against passing-off can be enforced against someone who copies the design applied to an article, especially if the article constitutes the get-up for another commodity, for example a powder compact or a bottle of wine. In such cases the protection would be indefinitely long (and automatic) but it is one of the prerequisites for a successful passing-off action that the plaintiff's product be distinctive. In other words, a passing-off action would be bound to fail if the plaintiff cannot prove that the design applied to his product is well known throughout the UK and, what is more, known to be peculiar to only his product so that purchasers (the trade and the public) would automatically associate the product with him. The famous designs of the Coca Cola bottle and Haig's Dimple bottle readily fall into the category protected from passing-off because either of these bottles constitutes a container used as a distinguishing guise for its otherwise visually indistinguishable contents, that is to say a particular form or fashion of presentation of a drink which cannot otherwise be visually distinguished from drinks of the same or a different kind made by the same or other manufacturers.

A passing-off action was not long ago successful in the Court of Appeal, where the defendant sold capsules for a drug in the same size and distinctive black and green colour as the plaintiff's capsules. In fact, the capsules were identical except for different markings of the respective drug manufacturers' names. It was held that there had been passing-off since the goods had been sold long enough with this get-up to be recognized by the public as goods of a particular manufacturer, namely the plaintiff, even though the public may not have known the identity of the manufacturer.

In another case, where an interlocutory injunction to restrain passing-off was refused (but granted on the basis of a design registration) for a chair that had allegedly been infringed, the plaintiff argued that the shape of the defendant's chair was so close to the registered chair design that its very existence on the market would lead to confusion. Said the judge: 'If there is no false representation, there can be no passing-off, and the mere copying of the shape of the plaintiff's article is not itself such a representation'. The judge admitted, however:

> There might be a case where an article itself is shaped in an unusual way, not primarily for the purpose of giving some benefit in use or for any other practical purpose, but in order purely to give the article a distinctive appearance characteristic of the particular manufacturer's goods. In such an event it seems to me possible that such a manufacturer may be able in course of time to establish such a reputation in such distinctive appearance of the article itself as would give him a cause of action in passing-off if his goods were copied, because in the circumstances assumed the putting of the copy on the market would amount to a representation that it emanated from the plaintiff.

The author can envisage such a case, namely, the arrow-shaped clips on all 'Parker' writing implements. It seems probable that the Parker Pen Co. could have a cause of a passing-off action on the basis of these distinctive clips which enjoy a world-wide reputation.

In yet another case that came to trial, in respect of a furniture suite, it was repeated:

> The basic requirement in a passing-off action of the present type is that the plaintiff should have such a reputation in the goods in question that they are distinctive of him and are recognized as being so by the relevant members of the trade and public. It is only if the plaintiff succeeds first of all in

establishing this *sine qua non* requirement that he is able to go on to try to establish the further requirement that there has been a representation by the defendant that his goods are the goods of or connected with the plaintiff.

8.2 Private protection procedures

Owing to the expense of litigation in the High Court and the poor chances of being able to obtain interim relief by way of an injunction if the design registration in suit is a recent one or its validity is being disputed, a cheaper and allegedly more effective and rapid scheme for design protection has been devised by some trade associations for use by one member against another member. For example, in the furniture trade there is one particular association where a complaint of design infringement can be investigated by a committee and sanctions applied to the accused party if found guilty. The sanctions applied by some trade associations include expulsion from membership and debarment from participating in exhibitions. The author has no personal knowledge of the success of these private schemes but it is questioned whether sanctions provide satisfactory relief for a complainant and whether legally unqualified committees are competent to judge the issue in the first place. Of course, infringers who do not belong to the trade association remain unaffected.

8.3 Secrecy agreement

In section 2.29 it was recommended that designs should not be divulged to outsiders before a design application has been filed. The dangers are obvious, even if the disclosure is made in confidence. In these days of sophisticated industrial espionage and detective work, it is relatively simple for ideas, to put it mildly, to leak out. In addition, there is the difficulty of preventing departing employees from taking ideas with them for the benefit of the next employer. An employment contract with secrecy provisions might minimize but can certainly not eliminate this danger.

There is one circumstance in particular where total temporary reliance may have to be placed on a secrecy agreement and this is where the designer is unwilling or unable to spend money on one or possibly numerous design applications before he finds a company that is prepared to market the articles. In fact, the designer may be depending on an interested company to finance the design applications for him. This situation arises very frequently because

Britain is renowned for turning a deaf ear to innovators and, as previously described, it may take months of patient endeavours before an interested manufacturer is found. Indeed, it is not an exaggeration to say that often a matter of years elapse because, apart from the fact that an independent designer must earn a living and cannot devote all his time to the exploitation of his designs, manufacturers who have been approached take a long time to reply.

In the meantime, the British design application, if one was filed, will have been registered and published and the six month priority period for corresponding foreign design applications will have expired. It will therefore be too late to obtain valid design registrations in some countries by the time a manufacturer has been found who is prepared to accept the design and help the author to pay for foreign applications. If no British design application has yet been filed, the last opportunity to do so would be upon commercial acceptance of the design but any intervening publication would render the resulting registration invalid. To keep the danger of premature publication to an absolute minimum until a taker is found, it is therefore strongly recommended that the author should conclude a secrecy agreement with every manufacturer to whom he discloses his design. Such an agreement is often in the form of a letter and might read as follows:

> I have developed a musical instrument and have been advised that a valid design registration is obtainable for it both here and abroad in addition to the copyright which subsists in the instrument case, the operating instructions and certain accessories.
>
> In consideration of allowing you to inspect a prototype of the instrument with a view to assessing its commercial possibilities and negotiating an agreement for its commercial exploitation, please signify (by countersigning the duplicate of this letter) your agreement to keep secret all particulars and descriptions of the instrument and that you will not, without my authority, make any notes or copies describing the instrument and that, should the negotiations fail, you will return the prototype intact together with all notes and copies that were made with my consent.
>
> Your signature will also be regarded as confirmation of your understanding that, without my prior consent, neither you nor your employees or agents in so far that it is in your power

reasonably to prevent will make or use any copy of an instrument that may be based on the same idea; nor will you discuss the instrument except in private with me or such other persons as I may specify.

The above secrecy agreement is far from satisfactory and should not be relied on if it is at all possible to file a design application before the design is shown around.

8.4 Know-how licence

It should be borne in mind that on many occasions a manufacturer has more to give to a potential licensee than permission to make use of a registered design, namely details of manufacturing techniques, tooling, materials and perhaps even useful hints on marketing—in short, tricks of the trade or know-how. Very often this know-how is more valuable than a design registration or patent and it should be licensed specifically in addition to a licence on any design registration because a know-how licence can be kept in operation for very long after the design registration has already expired. The following are imaginary heads of agreement between a British company and a foreign concern which desires to be taught how to make similar products. Representatives of the respective companies negotiated satisfactory terms and at the end of the day signed these heads of agreement, leaving it to the solicitors to engross the full licence at their leisure.

Heads of Agreement for a know-how licence

made in London this . . . . day of . . . . 197 . . . .
between LEXIQUE LIMITED ('Lexique'), a British company of . . . . , on the other part.
and
FRITZ K. G. ('Licensee'), a Kommanditgesellschaft organized and existing under the laws of the Federal Republic of Germany, of . . . . , on the other part.

1. The signatories to this agreement, Herr Max Fritz and Mr George Myrants are sole proprietor and managing director of Licensee and Lexique, respectively, and are authorized to sign this document which shall be legally binding on their respective companies.

2. Lexique owns valuable information relating to the manufacture, by means of injection moulding machines, of educational toys

marketed by Lexique under the trade mark L E X I Q U E and expects in the future to come into the possession of further such information.

3. Lexique is the exclusive licensee throughout the world.
   (a) under artistic copyright subsisting in drawings of the toys and has the exclusive right to apply any design corresponding to the drawings to any article including the right to grant sub-licences,
   (b) under the design to be registered on UK design application No. 956,961 in respect of a particular such toy,
   (c) under any design registrations that may be sought abroad corresponding to the UK registration and will ensure that the exclusive licences (which Licensee has inspected) are maintained in force for their maximum terms.

4. Licensee shall have the exclusive manufacturing rights for the toys in the Federal Republic of Germany ('Germany') and be granted a corresponding licence for the know-how and royalty-free sub-licences in respect of the design registrations and copyright.

5. Lexique will assist Licensee to establish production of the toys in Germany.

6. Licensee shall have exclusive selling rights for the toys in an area ('territory') covering the following countries, namely Austria, Switzerland, Czechoslovakia, Federal Republic of Germany, Poland, Turkey and the USSR.

7. Lexique will supply on demand all specifications, working drawings and other drawings and information necessary to establish production of the best toys known to Lexique.

8. Lexique shall, before publication of the UK design registration or the drawing which is the subject of artistic copyright, arrange with the copyright and design author to apply for one or more German design registrations in respect of the toy. Licensee may recommend other countries within the territory where design protection should be sought, if such is available.

9. Lexique shall apply for registration of its trade mark L E X I Q U E at least in Germany and in other countries as may be agreed.

10. Lexique shall make available during setting-up of production the services of a professional engineer to advise and instruct Licensee, the engineer to be Mr George Myrants unless he be prevented from attending by force majeur.

11. The engineer's travelling expenses to and from Germany and living expenses and accommodation in Germany while rendering these services will be paid by Lexique during the first week (including rest days) and thereafter by the Licensee at the rate of £400 per week payable to Lexique for each week or part thereof.

12. Lexique will during the term of the agreement supply any further information relating to the manufacture of the toys that may come into Lexique's possession.

13. Lexique will, in respect of any of the further information that may be patentable or registrable, file or cause to be filed patent and/or design applications in any country of the territory that Licensee may demand and Licensee's exclusive manufacturing and selling rights shall extend to toys made in accordance with such patents and designs.

14. All the patent, design and trade mark applications to be filed will be prepared by Lexique's agents but the expenses shall be refunded by Licensee within two months of presentation of a copy of each debit note.

15. Lexique will not make or sell the toys in the territory or authorize or assist others so to do.

16. Licensee is required to be ready for production and submit production samples for Lexique's approval within 12 months from the date of these heads of agreement. Until Licensee is in a position to execute orders from its own production, Lexique is prepared to supply Licensee with the toys f.o.b. at a discount of 20 per cent of Lexique's then current net UK selling price, before VAT.

17. Licensee shall mark each toy with the appropriate design registration or patent number or all such numbers and with the designation © followed by the copyright owner's name and the year 1976.

18. Licensee will treat as confidential all as yet unpublished information supplied by Lexique and Lexique will do likewise with any unpublished information supplied by Licensee.

19. As consideration for the exclusive manufacturing and selling rights in the territory and for the information supplied and to be supplied and for the assistance given and to be given, Licensee shall pay to Lexique £10 000 on signing these heads of agreement and a royalty of 8 per cent of the net selling price of each toy in the design or manufacture of which any use is made of the copyright or design or information or assistance made available by Lexique or which is marketed under the trade mark LEXIQUE.

20. The royalty is payable by banker's draft within 30 days of each calendar quarter and is to be calculated on the number of toys made, even if not yet sold.

21. Proper accounts are to be kept and may be inspected by Lexique.

22. A minimum royalty of £15 000 is payable within two years of signing these heads of agreement and £20 000 per year thereafter.

23. The trade mark LEXIQUE is to be applied on and in relation to all the toys made by Licensee hereunder, together with a statement that the trade mark is the property of Lexique.

24. Lexique may periodically check the toys for quality and insist on improvements if inferior to Lexique's own products.

25. Licensee may not assign or license the rights hereunder.

26. The term of the engrossed agreement is to be five years from today, renewable for successive terms of three years each.

27. Disputes are to be settled by arbitration in London under the Rules of the International Chamber of Commerce.

At the risk of stating the obvious, it is emphasized that the above heads are no more than indicative of the kind of considerations that are encountered in practice. It is money well spent to have an expert in these matters sit in on the negotiations so that he can assist in drafting the terms and perhaps even be instrumental in negotiating a better deal for his client.

9. The future of design protection

It is of the essence of man's nature not to be satisfied with past technical and artistic achievements. We will always strive for improvements, particularly in relation to goods destined for the consumer market. In any case, our tastes change and this alone will prompt manufacturers to alter their products. It is therefore certain that the flow of new designs from the drawing board (and from the craftsman's hands) will never cease, and where there are new designs there will also be a continued desire to obtain protection for these designs against indiscriminate copying by competitors who do not take the time or trouble to conduct developmental work of their own.

What is not so certain is whether the registration system will survive in its present form or, for that matter, at all, in order to afford the required protection against copying. It cannot be denied that the good designing of products is of ever increasing importance to manufacturers and customers alike. A good design is no more expensive to apply than a bad one but requires more initiative, talent and effort to think up. It is therefore right that the creators of new designs should be given the opportunity of acquiring a limited monopoly for the results of their endeavours in return for an application or registration fee. To some extent the future of the registration system might be regarded as being dependent on political considerations. A Socialist government is clearly not as anxious to assist capitalistic industrialists as a Conservative government might be, although it must be emphasized that the merits of industrial property protection have been recognized and implemented in most Iron Curtain countries, including the USSR itself. It should also be mentioned that Conservative governments in the UK are likewise not exactly fast in introducing new or amending existing legislation on industrial property matters. Judging from the inactivity of successive governments in matters of industrial property legislation, one might assume that the present system is here to stay for very many more years, except perhaps with regard to the overlap between the design and copyright laws, but there are other political considerations involved, such as the desirability of conforming to international agreements and legislation to placate our Common Market partners (or to discriminate against competition from certain countries).

A new Departmental Committee was established quite some time ago to consider the law affecting designs and copyright. Its report has been received by the government but when this might be published, what its recommendations will be and when it is to be acted upon by the government is impossible to predict. Events that have occurred in recent years seem to show an international trend in favour of design registrations. Until 1975, the Netherlands and Luxembourg held out against providing any form of protection for industrial designs but they have now introduced the Benelux registration system. This would indicate that there is a lot to be said for registrations and that the UK might be well advised to keep the registration system. The US, with its famous anti-trust laws, has nevertheless retained the registration system.

Then there are the newly developing countries, who invariably introduce a design registration procedure and therefore clearly see an advantage in it. In recognizing the desirability of extending the registration procedure to developing countries, the World Intellectual Property Organisation has prepared a model design registration law which aroused considerable interest. Even the South American countries who are taking measures to safeguard local industries from foreign dominance and competition are retaining the design registration procedure. New design registration law was recently introduced in Finland, Norway, Denmark and Sweden. The Federal Republic of Germany, which grants more design registrations annually than all the other countries in the world put together but whose registration procedure is more akin to a deposit system without a novelty search, has never deemed it necessary to provide a more effective registration system. The deposit system and the generous German law against unfair competition as well as a Utility Model Registration system for what one might call functional designs developed as a result of exercising a certain amount of inventive ingenuity and might all possibly be adopted in the UK one day, especially if this is expedient for conforming with future EEC laws.

Let us consider the circumstances as they exist in the UK at the present time. It is generally thought that the 1968 Copyright Act, affording a measure of automatic copyright protection for artistic industrial designs, was a mistake and overtures are being made to rectify the position but it could be that the law is here to stay and that the design registration system will one day be abolished altogether in favour of Utility Model registrations, the existing copyright law and perhaps a new law against unfair competition. Published figures seem to indicate that, in the not too distant future, there will be more foreign than UK applicants for British design registrations. Should this come about, it is indeed likely that there will be an active lobby advocating that the cost of maintaining a registration system is not justified for the benefit of a majority of non-nationals.

It must be admitted that those manufacturers who take any interest at all seem to have come to terms with the Design Copyright Act as it is now construed and applied. A notable exception is the spare parts industry, which cannot get used to the idea that copyright subsists in drawings and, if a manufacturer makes a spare part for someone else's machine, he could be infringing copyright. If one views this effect without bias, the conclusion must surely be reached that there is nothing unfair about leaving the market to the originator. Why should a UK manufacturer be able to make and sell replicas of components for machines developed in, say, Japan? The Japanese are capable of making and selling their own replacement parts; if they are not, they can soon license a British firm to make authorized copies but no one ought to be free to copy somebody else's design without paying for the privilege. To this extent, good luck to the Design Copyright Act, even though it has introduced anomalies and difficulties and is therefore far from pleasing. It has done nothing to remove the anomaly of affording 15 years of protection to some designs and 50 years plus to others. Also, there should not be double protection under the design law and the copyright law. It would be better for the registration system to go if copyright must absolutely stay, but in that case infringement should not be dependent on copying.

For the moment, however, we still have the design registration procedure and manufacturers should take advantage of what it has to offer until such time as the benefits of registration might become outpriced by an increase in the official fees prompted by the fact that the machinery that is maintained for granting design registrations is not being fully utilized.

A word about rewards to designers and inventors. Representations have recently again been made for a system of allowing innovators to share in the benefits of their innovations. At present, the ownership of a design or invention in the UK is governed by the employee's service contract. Nothing is laid down by statute concerning adequate reward for the employee; the service contract or the employer's generosity are here relied on.

Basically, the author fails to see why a designer or inventor should be rewarded in addition to his normal salary if similar provision is not also made for the inventors of new trade marks, the devisers of unpatentable but nevertheless useful improvements to existing machinery, processes, systems, lay-outs, the authors of artistic copyright, and so on. In other words, it is believed that inventors and designers should be treated no better nor worse than any other employee who contributes usefully to the progress of his employer's business. The employee's overall usefulness should desirably be reflected in his salary but not compulsorily by way of enacting a law. There is really no room for a statutory award scheme.

True, there are inventors and designers who attempt to obtain protection in their own name for something that rightfully belongs to their employers. When told that they would merely be holding the rights in trust for their employers, they abandon the attempt but they make no effort to let the employers have the benefit of the innovations because they allegedly would not be rewarded for their efforts. As a result, in a very few instances the employers, the industry and the country as a whole suffer a certain loss. A law could prevent this from happening by prescribing a compulsory award scheme but it is believed that the obstacles and objections are too numerous.

The compulsory award would have to depend on the usefulness of the innovation to the employer. This is often unknown until long after the idea was conceived. Hence, there would need to be provision for subsequent adjustment of the award in cases where it is a lump sum payment instead of on an annual royalty basis. But an innovator can hardly be expected to repay an award that was made and spent several years earlier. Consequently, adjustment could be made to work only one way, i.e., in the case of underpayment to the employee. A compulsory reward would also need to take into account the degree of originality or thought or ingenuity that was expended by the employee. This is actually done for compulsory awards in Germany but it is a very difficult, if not impossible, quantity to measure and is even more complicated if, to be fair, the contributory ideas and guidance by other employees and the management are taken into account.

As in Germany, the innovator's salary would also have to be a deciding factor in assessing the amount of the award. The author believes that, to be practical, this should be the one and only measure for any scheme of compulsory awards that may be introduced in this country but preferably the scheme for statutory awards should be abandoned once and for all.

Finally, will there ever be a single European or Common Market design registration to take the place of separate design registrations in each country? The author definitely thinks so and makes the guess that it will come into being before the end of this century. A European patent is almost an established fact, the building for the European Patent Office nearing completion in Munich. We are also on the threshold of a European trade mark registration insofar that the drafting of a suitable law has progressed to an advanced stage and the UK plans to make a strong bid for having the administering authority in its territory. In such a climate of international cooperation, the creation of a European design protection procedure is more than just conceivable within the next 20 years.

Appendix

Some time after the manuscript for this book had been sent to the printer, the Departmental Committee report referred to in Chapter 9 (presented to Parliament in March 1977) was published in HM Stationery Office (Cmnd 6732). It makes interesting reading for practitioners and students, analyses the present laws in depth, and makes noteworthy recommendations for improvement.

The Committee first met in February 1974. Its terms of reference were to consider and report whether any, and if so what, changes are desirable in the law relating to copyright as provided in particular by the Copyright Act 1956 and the Design Copyright Act 1968, including the desirability of retaining the system of protection of industrial designs provided by the Registered Designs Act

1949. The Committee discovered that 'a majority of people find the law as it stands complex and confusing. There has also been disclosed a considerable ignorance of the present law relating to these subjects.'

The report is excellent and easy to read but, regrettably, only of academic interest until such time as Parliament decides to act on the recommendations put forward. The following summary of the Committee's principal recommendations is offered by way of a supplement to Chapter 9. The Committee investigated copyright law as a whole, but the following points are confined to aspects relating to the protection of industrial designs and, even then, do not represent a complete summary. There are many paragraphs of interest in the body of the report and reflected in the recommendations, which can only be understood by reading the report as a whole, or at least the conclusions that prompted the final specific recommendations.

(a) For the designs of articles which will be bought because they are of pleasing appearance, at least the aesthetic elements of the designs should be protected automatically under the law of copyright for 25 years from the date of first marketing, but damages should be recoverable only if notice to the claim of copyright was given, such as by marking the articles.

(b) For the designs of articles to which no decorative addition has been made to influence the purchaser, two members of the Committee favour exclusion from copyright protection altogether, four members favour exclusion from copyright protection as for the designs of articles with aesthetic appeal and three members favour protection only under a proposed new copyright deposit system for 15 to 25 years.

(c) The present registration system granting a monopoly in a design should be abolished.

Index

207

Printed in Great Britain by J. W. Arrowsmith Ltd., Bristol